BASKETBALL *The Woman's Game*

MARYALYCE JEREMIAH
HEAD COACH WOMEN'S BASKETBALL
INDIANA UNIVERSITY

A SPORTS
PUBLICATION BY
THE ATHLETIC
INSTITUTE

Published by The Athletic Institute
200 Castlewood Drive
North Palm Beach, Florida 33408
Printed in the United States of America

Library of Congress Catalog Card Number 82-74327
ISBN 0-87670-069-5

A WORD FROM THE PUBLISHER

THIS SPORTS PUBLICATION, is but one item in a comprehensive list of sports instructional aids, such as video cassettes, 16mm films, 8mm silent loops and filmstrips which are made available by The Athletic Institute. This book is part of a master plan which seeks to make the benefits of athletics, physical education and recreation available to everyone.

The Athletic Institute is a not-for-profit organization devoted to the advancement of athletics, physical education and recreation. The Institute believes that participation in athletics and recreation has benefits of inestimable value to the individual and to the community.

The nature and scope of the many Institute programs are determined by a Professional Advisory Committee, whose members are noted for their outstanding knowledge, experience and ability in the fields of athletics, physical education and recreation.

The Institute believes that through this book the reader will become a better performer, skilled in the fundamentals of this fine event. Knowledge and the practice necessary to mold knowledge into playing ability are the keys to real enjoyment in playing any game or sport.

Howard J. Bruns
President and Chief Executive Officer
The Athletic Institute

D. E. Bushore
Executive Director
The Athletic Institute

ACKNOWLEDGMENTS

The author wishes to acknowledge and express appreciation to the following people who contributed to the completion of this book: Mary Schumacher for typing the manuscript, Ann Lawver for taking the photographs, Mike Rose and Dick Beikman for developing the photographs, and a special thanks to Sue Watts, Rachelle Bostic, Missy Leckie, and Denise Jackson, members of Indiana University's women's basketball team, for helping with the photographs.

DEDICATION

To My Nieces, Tammi, Denise, Jan, Amanda and Jennifer

TABLE OF CONTENTS

KEY TO DIAGRAMS

〜〜〜〜 Dribble

▬▬▬▬▬ Path of Ball

•••••••••••••••• Path of Player

Introduction

Girls and women all over the world are playing the game of basketball. Basketball — a game that has typically and uniquely been a "man's game" is being taken by storm by eager young female athletes who are finding the same excitement in scoring a jumper, stealing a pass, leaping for a rebound as have their brothers and fathers.

Because the last decade has seen such a tremendous growth in the sport for women, there is an equally tremendous need for girls to be taught the fundamentals of the game while they are young. Many opportunities are waiting for these female athletes as they enter high school and go on to college. High school competition is becoming highly developed with state championships, college scouting service listings, international opportunities and community programs.

Colleges all over the U.S. have full scholarships available to the female basketball player who has perfected her skill to a high level. National championships are now the ultimate goal for major collegiate basketball programs.

Because of the interest and growth in women playing basketball, many avenues of learning and skill development have been created in addition to the school setting. Summer camps for girls as young as nine years of age are doing a booming business. Community summer leagues (like the traditional little leagues for boys) are growing, and boys and girls are playing the game together on the playgrounds of many major cities.

With all this growth, however, there remains an area that is still quite deficient for girls and women in basketball. That area is the **written means of communication. There are very few books or articles — compared to the men's productivity — written specifically for the women's game.

Perhaps the **reason** for this is **twofold. First,** there are not many women who are writing in this field and **second,** and perhaps even more to the point, there are very few differences in basketball for men and women today. The differences lie mainly in a few rules and even those depend on the level of the game.

Basketball: The Women's Game is a book written specifically for the young girl who aspires to be a successful basketball player. It will be helpful also to the youngster who loves to play the game recreationally. The purpose of the book is to present the very basic **individual** fundamentals in word and picture in such a way that the player can improve her own skill during her practice sessions.

The book is divided into three sections. The first section, defense, depicts the basic individual defensive skills necessary to become a good defensive player. Its purpose also is to motivate and convince players of the absolute necessity of being dedicated at the defensive end of the court.

Section two, **offense,** also outlines the simple and basic skills necessary to be a successful offensive player. This section attempts to show the young player the many different skills there are for her to continually practice.

The third section explains the importance of practicing regularly and also shows some specific practice activities available for her. Methods of warming up and necessary equipment are also detailed.

Basketball is fast becoming a major sport for girls and women. It's exciting, skillful, and very enjoyable for participant and spectator alike. **Basketball: The Women's Game** is one more facet of its phenomenal growth. It should be read and used as a check list and evaluation tool for anyone who wants to improve her skill. It is easy to read and is illustrated so that the reader can **see** the mechanics of the skills. It, like any tool, is helpful only when used. Use it to build your game.

SECTION ONE

Defense:
The Secret to Success

DEFENSE: THE SECRET TO SUCCESS

The favorite part of basketball for most players is scoring. Seeing and hearing the ball ''swish'' through the nets to the sounds of cheers keeps many a young player at the game. How many points scored is an item of interest to all players. Newspapers print it, television announcers praise it, and parents are proud of it.

Even though the team that scores the most points definitely wins the game, the **key to success is** not offense but rather **defense.**

Why is this the key? Because **every** player can be a **good** defensive player and not every player can become a good offensive player — and therein lies the key to consistent success for a team as well as an individual. To keep the other team from scoring can very well mean the game — especially when your team is not doing so well offensively.

To become a good defensive player you need one basic ingredient — **DESIRE.** You must really want to be good defensively. The skills themselves are not that difficult — but neither are they all that fans admire. Each player's success on defense depends a great deal on how much she **wants** to do the job.

You have to be 100% sold on this part of the game. You have to be completely dedicated to improving your defense and practicing the skills outlined in this book. If you approach defense as something you do while you wait for the ball, you will be totally ineffective. But if you believe that keeping the opponent from scoring is the key to success you will play defense much more aggressively — a necessary ingredient to being effective.

The following defensive skills are basic to the game of basketball. Believe in their importance and practice them every time you play and whether or not you are a good shooter, you will have the key to your success — **DEFENSE.**

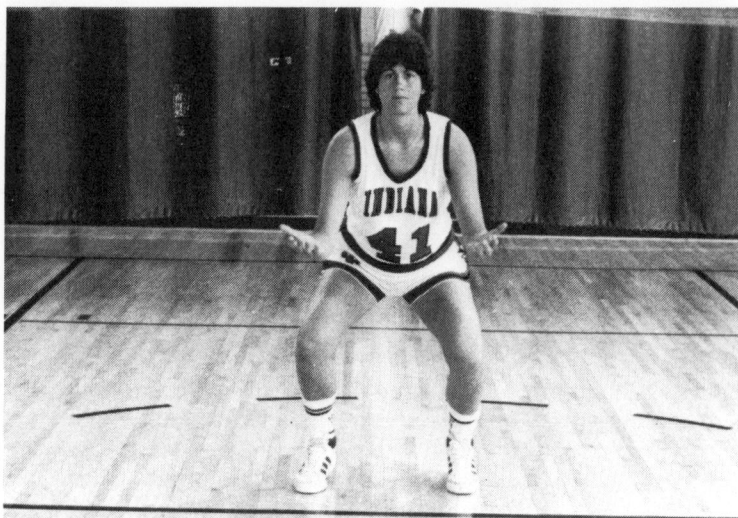

Illus. 1

STANCE

The defensive stance is the most basic skill in all defense.

FEET —	Shoulder width apart and square
KNEES —	Bent as in half-sitting position
ARMS —	Extended outside knees
PALMS —	Up
HEAD —	Up
EYES —	Able to see the ball at all times — not watching it but able to see it and your opponent.

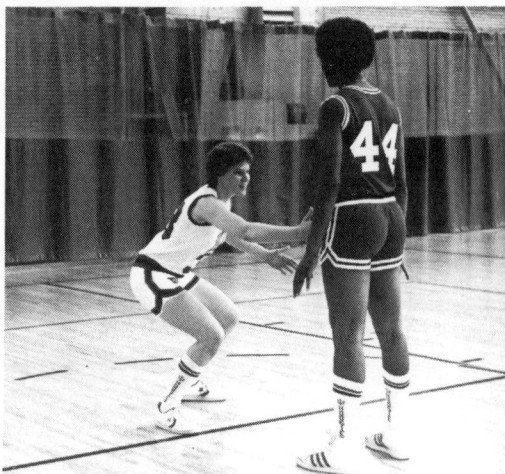

Illus. 2

4

DISTANCE FROM OPPONENT

You should be arms length away from your opponent **if** she has the ball but has not dribbled, passed, or shot. If you reach out you should be able to touch her belt buckle.

AGAINST THE DRIBBLE

Taking a Step Back

It is important to be ready for your opponent if she chooses to dribble the ball in an attempt to drive toward the basket. When this happens your first step should always be **back**, not forward or toward her.

This step back should be taken with the **inside** foot. The inside foot is determined by drawing an imaginary line from basket to basket. The foot closest to this line is your inside foot. (Illus. 3 and 4). In the

Illus. 3

Illus. 4

diagram below (Illus. 5) if you are playing defense at the "A" end of the court and you are on the right side of the court as you face the half line (**X-1**), the inside foot is the **left** foot. **X-2's** inside foot is her **right** foot.

At the "B" end of the court **X-3's** inside foot is her **right** foot and **X-4's** inside foot is her **left** foot.

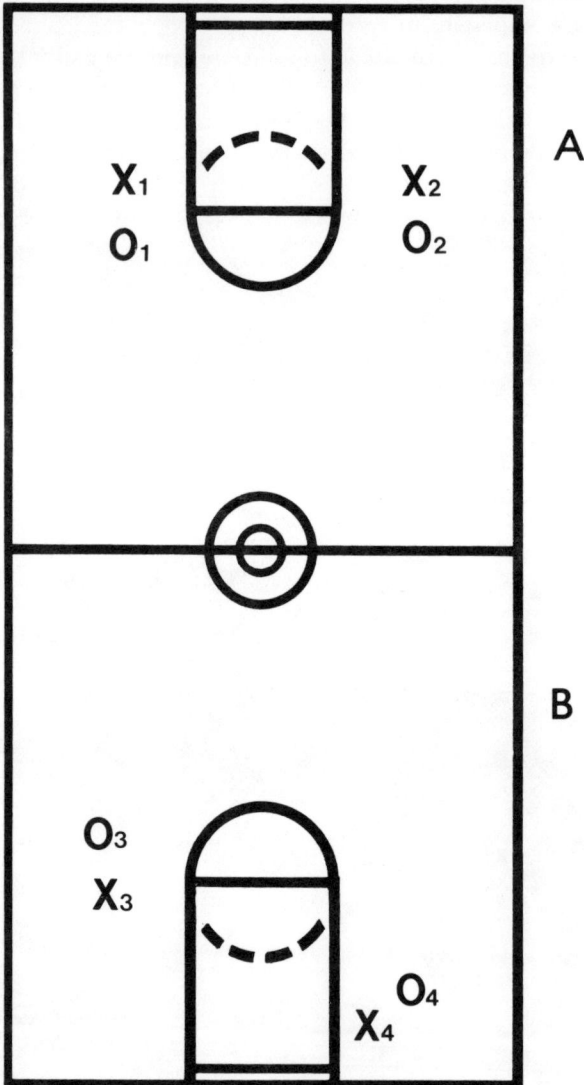

Illus. 5

When the dribbler puts the ball down to make a move toward the basket, the step back is taken with the inside foot. The second step is taken with the other foot and is wide. **The closer you get to the basket, the closer you should be to your opponent.** (Illustrations 6-9 show defense against the dribble to the defense's right and Illustrations 10-12 going to the left).

Illus. 6

Illus. 7

Illus. 8

Illus. 9

Illus. 10

Illus. 11

Illus. 12

USING YOUR HANDS

Your hands can be a great help to you on defense. They should always be out with **palms up** and they should always be moving. **Do not reach** toward the ball so much that it pulls you off balance but as the player is dribbling the ball and as she brings it between the two of you, if your hands are constantly moving and **"swatting"** at the ball, the offense will almost give you the ball. (Illus. 13-14)

Illus. 13

Illus. 14

SEEING THE BALL

At this point it should be emphasized that the center of every basketball game is the **BALL**. Every good player should tell herself that during **every** game she should **see** the ball. You do not do this by turning your head every time the ball moves but rather you see the ball by using **peripheral vision** or seeing it out of the corner of your eye.

Many defensive errors are made because players are busy looking for the other participants and losing sight of the ball. **Know where the ball is at all times.** If you focus on this skill, it can help you if you should **lose sight** momentarily of the **player** you are guarding. The opposite of this is **not as true.** That is, if you focus on your player, it probably **will not help** you to **find the ball** if you should lose sight of it momentarily.

In Illustration 15 you can see how proper positioning on the court can help you to see your opponent and the ball. Take a step back from the line between the ball and the player you are guarding and you can see both. These positionings create a triangle of **you, me and the ball.**

AGAINST THE PASS

When your player receives the ball, she can do one of three things — pass, dribble, or shoot. You already know you must take a step back with the inside foot if she decides to dribble. She now has two choices — passing or shooting. If she is too far away from the basket you can be sure she will want to pass the ball.

If the player tries to pass, you can defend against this by being as close to her as possible (Illus. 16) with one hand up and one hand on the ball or as close to being on it as possible. In other words, **crowd** your opponent, be all over her **without** fouling her and, with the correct use of your hands, prevent the pass from being made easily.

By being aggressive toward your opponent after she has picked up her dribble, you not only are playing good defense on your opponent, but you are also helping to keep the ball from being passed to someone who may be closer to the basket and in a more advantageous position to shoot.

Remember — (1) **arms length away before** dribble, pass or shoot, (2) one step back if a **drive** is attempted, and (3) crowd or get all over the opponent the second the dribble is **picked up.**

Illus. 15

AGAINST THE SHOT

Many players get great thrills from blocking shots and if done correctly and effectively, shot blocking can be lots of fun. However, the number of times a player blocks a shot without fouling is minimal. Defense against a shot has two basic phases. The **first** one involves attempting to prevent the shot from being taken.

This is done by immediately crowding the player when she has picked up the dribble. (Illus. 17). The closer you can play to a player and **not get beat** to the basket the more chance you have to prevent a shot being taken.

If you have one hand up and one hand on the ball it is difficult for your opponent to shoot the ball. If you hesitate **or** if you are too far away from the shooter, she will get the shot off even if you have your hands and arms in the correct position. In other words, you will be too late to prevent the shot.

The other phase is defending or blocking the shot when it is taken. Illustration 18 shows the correct technique to be used when attempting to block a shot. The following should be executed:

1.   If the ball is shot with the **right hand** — the defensive block should be with the **right hand.**
2.   If the ball is shot with the **left hand** — the defensive block should be with the **left hand.**

Illus. 16   Illus. 17   Illus. 18

3. The follow-through is to the **side of the body of the shooter.**
4. Never attempt to block a shot while playing square to the shooter unless you can follow through to the **side** of the shooter.

If you are considerably shorter than the player who is shooting, all chances of successfully blocking her shot are small. The better alternative to blocking a shot is for you to stand as close to the shooter as you can with both hands raised as high over your head as possible (Illus. 17), thus causing at least a distraction to the shooter.

Defense against the dribble, pass and shot are related to each other. They all begin with the correct defensive stance — **staying low** to be able to move quickly and staying as close as possible yet far enough away to prevent a pass or shot and also to keep from getting beat to the basket.

This defense is what you **must** be able to play if you are to become a good one-on-one player. It is basic to all the rest of the defensive skills that will be pictured and discussed in this book. It is basic to the entire defensive phase of basketball and it can be practiced every time you have a ball, a hoop, and one opponent to play with.

It demands the desire to work on it every time you play. You cannot overlook it and let it go so that you can work on your offense. You cannot proceed to the next phase of defense successfully until you have learned to be successful with one-on-one defense. It demands practice and thinking each time you play.

ONE-PASS-AWAY DEFENSE

One-pass-away defense means that you are guarding a player to whom the ball may be passed. Of course this **could** be any of the players but most frequently it is the player(s) closest to the ball. The diagram below shows how you can determine if you are one pass away. (Illus. 19)

Defense at this position is very similar to that of the player defending the ball. You should be in a low defensive stance with your inside hand in the **passing lane** (that area between your player and the ball). Your inside foot can be a little toward the basket. You should be about 1/2 step farther from your player than you would be if she had the ball.

If you know you are quicker than the player you are guarding, you can be closer to her. The guide to use is this: **BE AS CLOSE AS YOU CAN TO GET INTO "ON-THE-BALL" DEFENSE** as quickly as possible. If you are quicker, this position will be closer than if you are of even speed or slower than your player.

X-*2* and **X**-*3* are one-pass-away defensive players when the ball is at the top of the Key. If **X**-*2's* player has the ball, **X**-*1* and **X**-*5* are one pass away. If **X**-*3's* player has the ball, **X**-*4* and **X**-*1* are one-pass away defensive players. If **X**-*4's* player has the ball, **X**-*3* is one pass away and if **X**-*5's* player has the ball, **X**-*2* is one pass away.

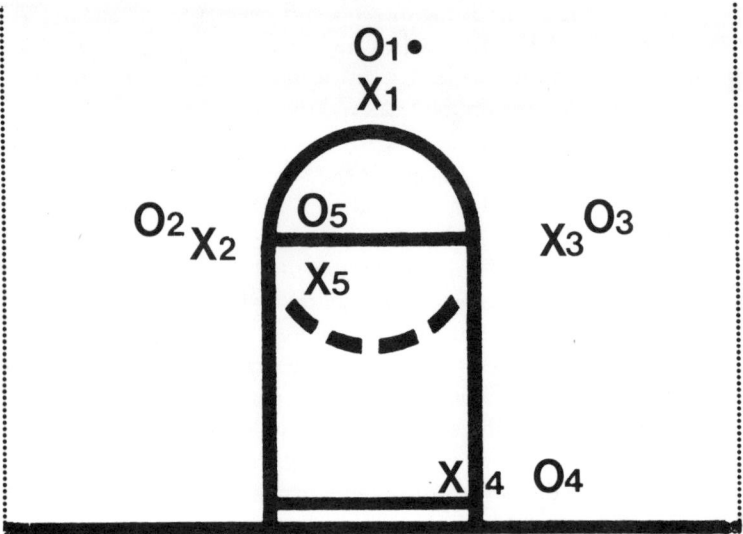

Illus. 19

Illus. 20

You may be able to actually deny the pass or keep your player from receiving the ball by extending your inside hand into the passing lane. (Illus. 20) If you are guarding a player who is very close to the basket and is also one pass away, your position will be different. (This will be illustrated in defense against the post.)

Whether you are one pass, two passes, or more away from your player, the rule to follow is: THE FARTHER YOU ARE AWAY FROM **THE BALL**, THE FARTHER AWAY YOU CAN BE FROM **YOUR PLAYER**. Remember, however, you must be able to get in ball-denial position by the time the ball is received by your player.

TWO PASSES AWAY

The diagram below shows when you are two passes away from the ball. If the ball is in **X-1**'s position, **X-4** and **X-5** are two passes away. Their position should be two steps, at least, back from their opponent and back a step toward the basket so they can see their player **and** the ball. This is called **opening** up to the ball.

If the ball is in **X-2**'s position, **X-3** and **X-4** are two passes away and should be opened up to the ball also. Every time the ball moves, **every** defensive player should move because their positions from the ball change. If you understand this principle in relation to the ball, you will be in proper position and able to cover your responsibilities.

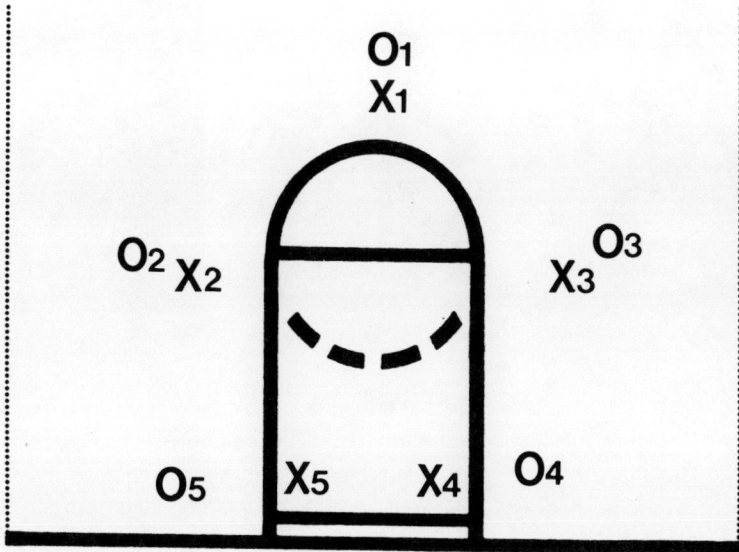

Illus. 21

AT THE BASELINE

Defending your player when she tries to drive the baseline is one of the simpler places to play defense yet causes many players a lot of problems. If you are playing at the wing position (free throw line extended) and your player makes a driving move to the basket, your defensive moves should be as follows:

1. Take **first step** back with inside foot. (Illus. 22)
2. Slide baseline with opposite foot or **second step.** (Illus. 23)
3. The third step should slide so that you are square to your opponent and **straddling the baseline.** (Illus. 24)

The **baseline** itself can be of great help to a good defensive player if she will use it to her advantage. It serves as another ''defensive'' player as it cuts off the offensive player and eliminates an option.

The most common error is not squaring to the offense and turning so you are **facing** the baseline instead of the offense. This allows the player with the ball to drive clear down the baseline.

If you are square to her, straddling the line, and you get there before she does, you have created a potential charging situation, **or** the player will have to pick up her dribble, **or** will have to change direction and go **inside** where there will be more defensive players to help you. Remember: ONE STEP BACK, SLIDE, STRADDLE BASELINE.

Illus. 22   Illus. 23   Illus. 24

AGAINST THE POST

The closer the ball gets to the basket, the more dangerous it is for the defense because it is easier to score. Therefore, defending in the post area (Illustration 25) becomes very strategic. A very good rule to follow is this: NEVER ALLOW YOUR PLAYER TO GET THE

BALL IN THE POST AREA. If you allow her to get the ball you will be faced with a most difficult defensive situation and will risk the very real possibility of fouling and/or allowing two points.

In Illustrations 26-28 you can see a player coming from the opposite side of the floor to receive a pass in the post area. The defensive player's job is to keep the offensive player from receiving that pass. She does that by:

1. **Playing away** from her player **before** the move is started. (Illus. 26)

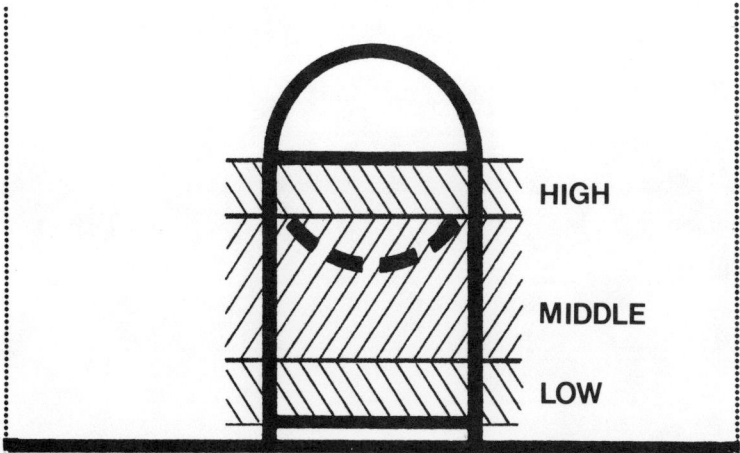

HIGH

MIDDLE

LOW

Illus. 25

Illus. 26

2.   When the move is started, the defender merely beats the offensive player to the spot. (Illus. 27)

3.   Playing in front of the offensive player in the key area. (Illus. 28)

4.   Keeping one hand high to prevent a successful pass. (Illus. 28)

Any time a player moves from the "**off-ball**" side of the court (the side opposite the ball) to the "**ball**" side of the court (the side of the ball) her responsibility is **beat them to the spot.** If you are playing off them to begin with, this makes the job much easier.

Illus. 27

Illus. 28

When an offensive player posts up (turns and faces the ball with back to the basket) in the low position on the ball side, the defender must immediately get in front of the offensive player. This is done by stepping or hooking your leg around the offensive player's and fighting for that position.

Middle post defense (see Illustration 25 for location) is played in a very similar manner as low post defense. You do not want the ball to be received by your player in this position. You have to be ready to move quickly and always be in proper position to your player **in relation to the ball** as explained earlier.

High post defense is played differently because here you are 13-15 feet away from the basket and in a percentage area (shots that have the best chance to go in). The best defensive position for this area of the floor, if you are guarding a post player, is to play behind her and discourage or deny the pass by moving your hand and arm around her as shown in Illustration 29.

You play behind her here so that if she receives the pass and turns to face the basket you are ready to prevent the drive, pass, or shot by being in the basic stance and in a low position.

The most difficult post area defense to play is when a player cuts from the outside (ex., from the top of the circle) to receive a pass. Your goal should still be to keep her from getting the ball and you need to be aware of this possibility at all times.

1. Stay low and ready.
2. When your player passes, take a quick step back.

Illus. 29

17

3.   When she starts to move into the lane be in front of her.

The following are simple basic rules to follow when considering defense at different positions.

1.   When playing defense **outside the lane,** stay **between player and basket.**

2.   When playing defense **inside the lane,** stay in **front of player** — between her and the ball.

3.   When playing defense **against a post player,** play **behind** when she is **high** — play in **front** when she is in **middle** or **low.**

4.   Remember, defense is playing at different speeds and sometimes you must accelerate to be in the correct position.

5.   The **ball** is the focus of the game. Know where it is every second.

THE DEFENSIVE REBOUND

Well over 50 percent of all shots taken do not go in and the team who rebounds these shots is usually the team who wins games. Defense ordinarily has the goal of keeping the opponents from shooting but this of course is impossible every time down the floor. If, however, a shot is attempted, defense should **never** allow the offense to get the rebound and attempt another shot. Rebounding then becomes one of the most important aspects of the game.

A good rebounder is a player who first of all **wants** to be a good rebounder. It is often true that the player who **thinks** rebound all the time **gets** rebounds even though she may be smaller and even slower. If you wait until the ball is shot before you think about rebounding the ball, you will not be a contributing rebounder.

A good rule to keep in mind when practicing to be a good defensive rebounder is this: **DEFENSE IS NOT OVER UNTIL THE BALL IS REBOUNDED BY THE DEFENSIVE TEAM.** In other words, you must continue to **contain** your player until your team has the ball. If you do not do this, the offensive team will more than likely rebound the ball and you will have to continue to play defense. This containment is called **blocking out** and is discussed in the next section.

When you do rebound the ball, there are several things to keep in mind to make it a good rebound:

1.   Jump as high as you can. A running start or a step or two to the basket will help if you are away from the basket.

2.   Grab the ball with both hands at the very top of your jump. (Illus. 30)

3.   Try to make your body as wide as you can by spreading your

legs in the air (this is a difficult part of the rebound but if practiced can become habit). This position keeps opponents farther away from you. (Illus. 31)

4. Once you have the ball, try to protect it by pulling the ball into your body and keeping your elbows out.

5. Hang on to it tightly as others may try to swat it from your grasp.

Illus. 30   Illus. 31

BLOCKING OUT — INSIDE AND OUTSIDE

When the ball has been shot or is in the process of being shot, you need to keep your player behind you so that you have the inside position to go to the ball.

There are two ways your player can go to try and rebound the ball — **inside** (toward the foul lane) or **outside** (toward the end line). Illus. 32)

If your player moves toward the **inside**:

1. You take a step toward the player and make contact. (Illus. 33)
2. Pivot on your **inside** foot. (Illus. 34)
3. Keep her behind you by using your hips and body — legs spread wide. (Illus. 35)
4. Keep your arms up and out. (Illus. 35)
5. Make an aggressive move toward the ball.

An important phase of rebounding is making contact with the player. If you do not step toward her or allow her to contact you, even though you pivot correctly, she will probably go around you and get to the ball first.

If your player moves toward the **outside**:

1. Take a step toward your player. (Illus. 36)
2. Pivot on your outside foot. (Illus. 36)
3. Keep her behind you by using your hips and body — legs spread wide. (Illus. 37)

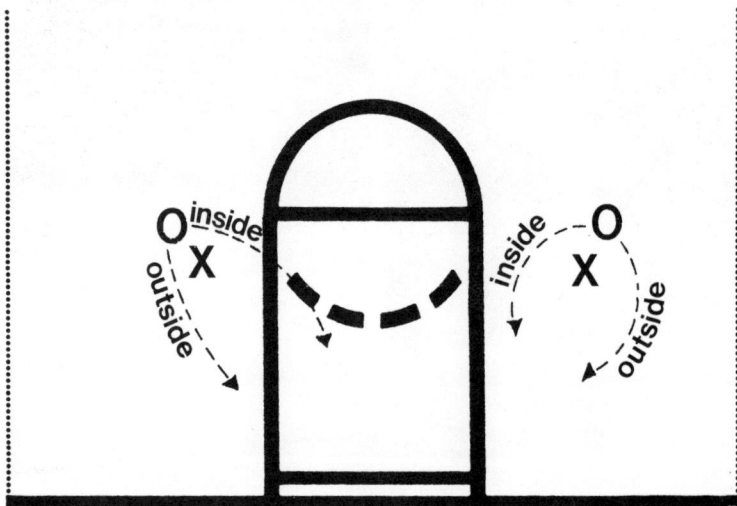

Illus. 32

4.   Keep your arms up and out. (Illus. 38)

5.   Make an aggressive move toward the ball.

Pivoting on the correct foot to block out is very important in being a good defensive rebounder because it enables you to **block the path** of the offensive player. If you learn it correctly it will become habit. If you try to block out just by turning around, you will find the offensive player will get around you more often. Remember **WANTING TO BE** A GOOD REBOUNDER IS THE FIRST NECESSARY REQUIREMENT TO BEING A GOOD REBOUNDER.

Illus. 33

Illus. 34

Illus. 35

Illus. 36

Illus. 37

Illus. 38

AGAINST PICKS AND SCREENS

Thus far we have discussed defense in a one-on-one situation. The fundamental skills necessary for **any** defensive situation begin with the **one-on-one** fundamentals. If these are not mastered, you will not be able to progress to two-, three- or five-player situations.

Since the **ball** is the center of the game, sometimes you will get blocked out or **screened out** by other players on the floor and in the process **your** player may get loose or by you.

Offensive players try to lose defensive players by using several different techniques. These will be illustrated in the offensive section of this book. If you are to be an overall **good defensive player,** you will need to know how to get around **picks** and **screens.**

A **pick** is a movement by an **offensive** player where she places her body so **close to a teammate's** defensive player that it allows her teammate to get a **clear path** either to the **basket** or to the **ball.**

A **screen** is a similar movement by an offensive player where she places her body **in the path** of a teammate's defensive player so that it allows her teammate to get a clear path either to the basket or the ball.

Defending these situations can be very difficult without the following being done by the defense:

1. **USE OF THE VOICE** — Defensive players need to learn to talk to each other and tell each other what is going on on the floor. If you see your teammate being picked or screened out, you should tell her by saying "pick right" or "pick left." This tells the teammate on which side of her the pick is being set.

2. **USE OF THE HANDS** — Use your hands to "feel" behind you so you can know when another player is close to you. It's a way of **seeing** without using your eyes.

3. **USE OF YOUR BODY** — You cannot be afraid to fight your way over and through these people. If you are afraid of contact in this situation you will be screened out easily.

4. **USE OF ANTICIPATION** — By knowing where the ball is at all times, it is often possible to anticipate when a screen or pick is going to be set and avoid it. In order to anticipate accurately you need to be thinking all the time.

There are three main ways to play defense against a pick or screen, namely **switching, sliding through,** and **going over the top.** All three are illustrated in the following pages.

SWITCHING

This defensive technique involves your **changing** offensive players with your teammate who has been screened or picked. In the diagram below, O-*1* sets a screen on X-*2*, clearing a path for O-*2*. Switching on defense involves X-*1* and X-*2* changing player to guard. X-*1* picks up O-*2* and X-*2* picks up O-*1*.

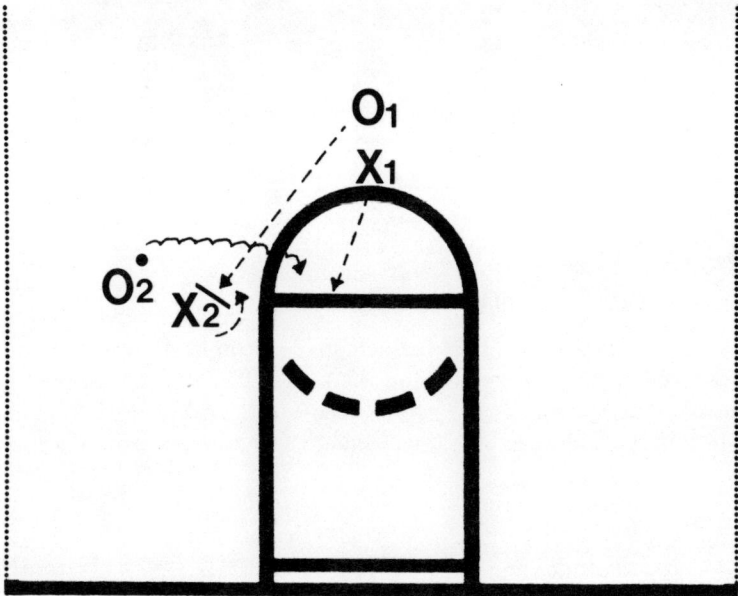

Illus. 39

If a switch is to be made, it must be **called** well in advance so it can be done quickly and in time for it to be completed. **Switching** is the **easiest way** to defend a pick but it also may not always be the best way. One of the disadvantages of this method is that when a switch is executed, the new players may be mismatched. That is, the new offensive player may be much bigger or much faster than the defensive player. (Illus. 40).

Another disadvantage of switching is that players try to switch back to their original opponents too soon and someone gets left unguarded. The point to remember here is this: IF YOU SWITCH, STAY SWITCHED UNTIL YOU CAN COMFORTABLY SWITCH BACK WITHOUT CONFUSION. This may mean you do not go back to your original player until the next time down the court. This is the only method of defending a pick or screen where you do not stay with your own player.

23

The new offensive player may be much bigger or much faster than the defensive player.

Illus. 40

SLIDING THROUGH

This technique involves the defensive person being screened going through the screen or behind the screen. The diagram below illustrates this technique. O-*1* gets a screen or pick on X-*2* and X-*2* stays with O-*2* by **sliding** to the **basket** side of O-*1*, thereby avoiding the effect of the pick.

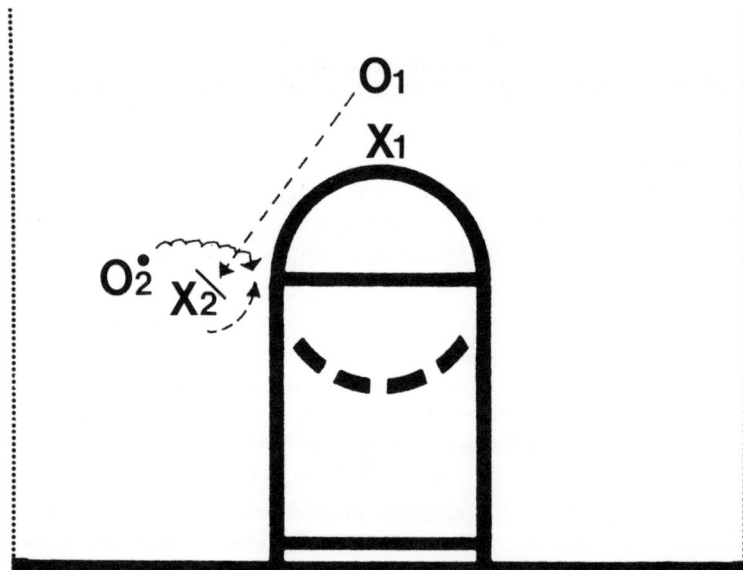

Illus. 41

24

If the pick is set tightly — that is very close to **X**-*2* — **X**-*2* will have to have adequate warning that **O**-*1* is coming in order to be able to execute the step back and to slide behind **O**-*1*. **X**-*1* continues to guard **O**-*1* and **X**-*2* stays with **O**-*2*. **Calling** the screen is of ultimate importance in this situation and it is **X**-*1*'s responsibility to call it for **X**-*2*.

A disadvantage of this method of defending the pick is that while **X**-*2* is sliding through, there is a moment when **O**-*1* is between **X**-*2* and **O**-*2*. At this moment the screen can actually be an effective screen because **O**-*2* can pull up and shoot behind **O**-*1*.

An important aspect of sliding through is anticipation and being ready by being in a good defensive stance so that you can fight through the screen. This takes **mental readiness** (as does the entire game) as well as **physical readiness.** It also demands a great deal of communication on the part of the whole team. (Illus. 42).

Illus. 42

GOING OVER THE TOP

The third method of defense against a pick or screen is both the most effective and most difficult method. In this technique intead of taking a step **back** or toward the basket, you take a step **toward the player** you are guarding in order to slide in **front** of the player setting the pick. In Illustration 43, **O**-*1* sets the pick or screen on **X**-*2* and **X**-*2* takes a step toward **O**-*2* and slides in front of **O**-*1* **or** goes over the top of **O**-*1*.

This again requires great anticipation, readiness, and verbal communication on the part of everyone. It is considered the best method because at no time is another player permitted between you and the player you are guarding. (Illus. 44)

One of the dangers, of this, however, is that in your attempt to get over the top you may crowd the offensive player so much that she will be able to drive to the basket (if she has the ball) or cut to the basket to receive a pass. If you keep in mind the first basic principles

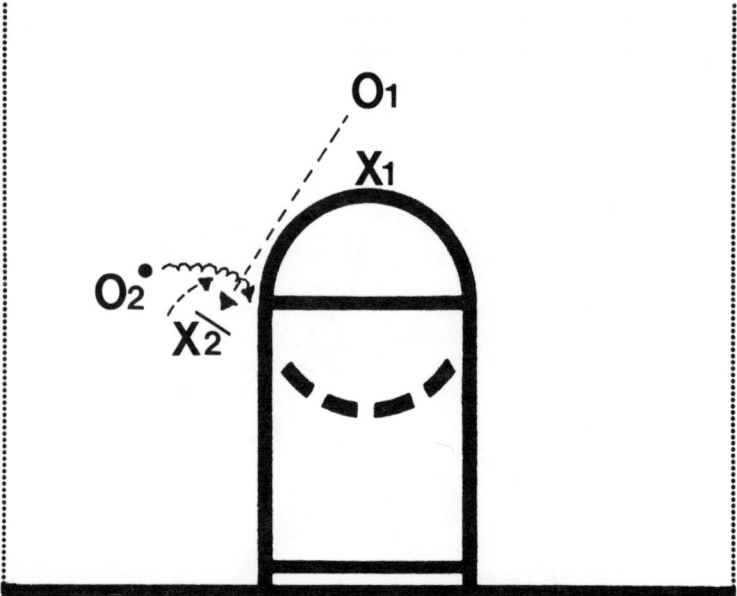

Illus. 43

Illus. 44

of defense in relation to distance from your player (arms length whenever possible if ball is not picked up) it will help you to avoid this danger.

In **summary** keep the following points in mind when defending against picks and screens:

1. Stay low, stay ready, know where ball is.
2. When **switching**, "switch" is called by players **not** being picked.
3. When **sliding through**, take a step back **toward the basket** and slide **behind** the pick — stay with your player
4. When **going over the top**, take step **toward your player** and slide **in front** of the pick — stay with your player.
5. Verbal communication is the key to success in defending against picks and screens.

Defending **screens** is done in the manner discussed above. The basic difference, as in the definition, is that a **screen** does not "pin" the defensive player as does a **pick**. You will have to be more aware of switching, sliding through or going over the top while you are **moving** because the objective of the offensive player will be to run you into the **screen** which is set in your **path** rather than right at your side. Your teammates will have to help you.

RACE TO CATCH UP

When you are guarding a player who gets by you and you find yourself behind her instead of in a good protective defense position, what should you do? The most natural thing for you to do is to reach for the ball and probably foul. The important thing to remember here is that **first** of all you have to **catch** the player before you can play defense against her.

To catch her you turn around, face the same direction she is facing, and race alongside her. She has the ball and you should be able to run faster **without** the ball than she can with it. This is a very common example of how important it is to play defense at different speeds throughout the game. A **sprint** is demanded in this situation and it becomes a simple foot race to get ahead of your opponent, enough to get in proper defensive position. **Turn around, sprint, get ahead, get into your stance.**

TEAM DEFENSE

Anything a **group** of people do, in this case a basketball team, will be only **as good as** the **individuals** making up the group or team. A **team** cannot play defense well if **each player** will not work hard and practice the individual defensive skills that have been outlined so far.

However, once each player has learned the skills or is in the process of learning and getting better each day, the team is ready to put all these skills together into a unit to play tough, aggressive defense.

It is at this point that a decision will be made as to the type of **team defense** your team will play. There are two **basic** kinds of team defenses: **PLAYER TO PLAYER** and **ZONE**. There are a number of variations of each of these but each is just a type of these two.

PLAYER-TO-PLAYER DEFENSE

Player-to-player defense is exactly what it is called. Each defensive player is assigned to guard a specific player on the other team. She stays with this player wherever she goes on the court and whereas the **ball** is always the center of the game, each defensive player is responsible for the player she is assigned.

The defensive skills you see in this book are skills necessary for **every** defense your team plays. They are used differently in zone defenses but player-to-player defense uses them in every defensive situation.

In Illustrations 45 and 46 player-to-player defense is shown with the ball in different positions. Note the variations in positions for one, two, three and four passes away from the ball. Notice that the farther away from the ball, the farther away is the defensive player.

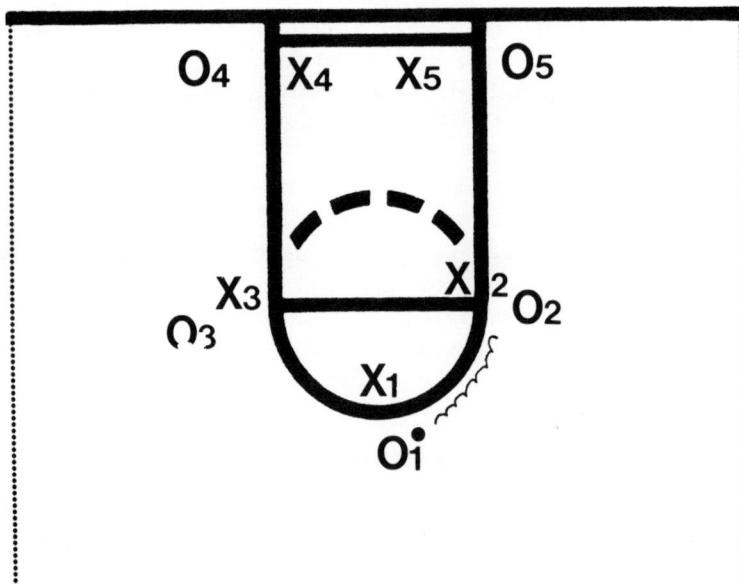

Illus. 45

In player-to-player defense you are responsible to be "on the ball" whenever the ball is close to you even if it means momentarily leaving your player to help out.

In Illustration 45 if O-1 dribbles the ball to her right, it is X-2's job to help on the ball. This should not be too difficult if she is in one-pass-away position to begin with.

In Illustration 46 if O-2 dribbles the ball to her left, it is X-1 and X-3's job to help on the ball. This principle works all over the floor and should be applied whenever possible.

In **player-to-player** defense remember:

1. The **ball** is the **focus** of the game. It is more important than your player, if a choice has to be made.
2. Every opportunity you have to help on the ball, you should do so.
3. Talk to each other constantly.
4. **Move** in proper relationships to your player **every time the ball moves.** Every pass and dribble requires **every** defensive player to move.
5. Player-to-player defense makes the offense shoot the ball close and prevents the outside shot.
6. Defense is not over until your team gets the ball. Rebound!

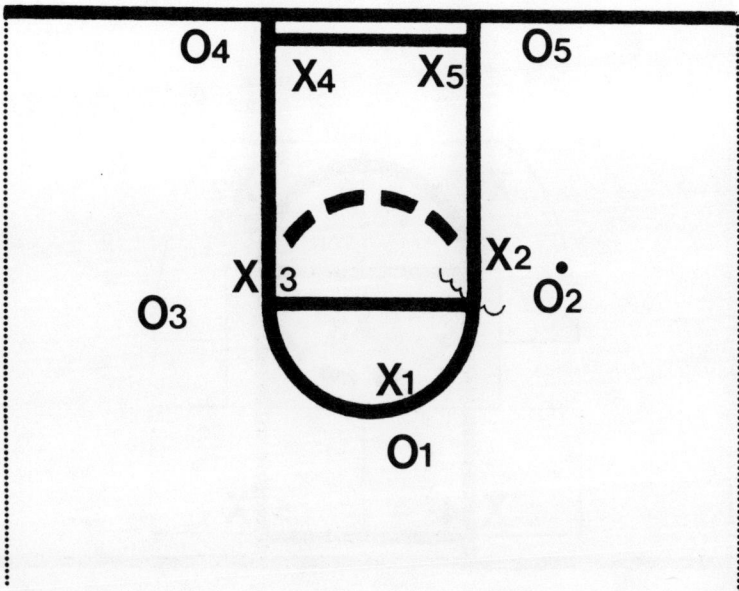

Illus. 46

ZONE DEFENSE

Zone defense is different from player to player, not that its **skills** are different but the **use** of these skills is different. Zones are based on **areas** of the floor rather than players. In a zone defense each player is **assigned** a **floor area** rather than a player.

When the ball is in your assigned area, you play player-to-player defense on the ball. Many players believe it is easier to play zone defense than man to man. NOT TRUE. You cannot play effective **zone defense** until and unless you have mastered the skills of **player-to-player defense.**

There are many different kinds of zones. One that lines up with two players at the top of the circle, one in the middle of the lane and two back by the baseline. This is called a 2-1-2 zone. (See Illustration 47.) The areas marked show each defensive player's assigned area.

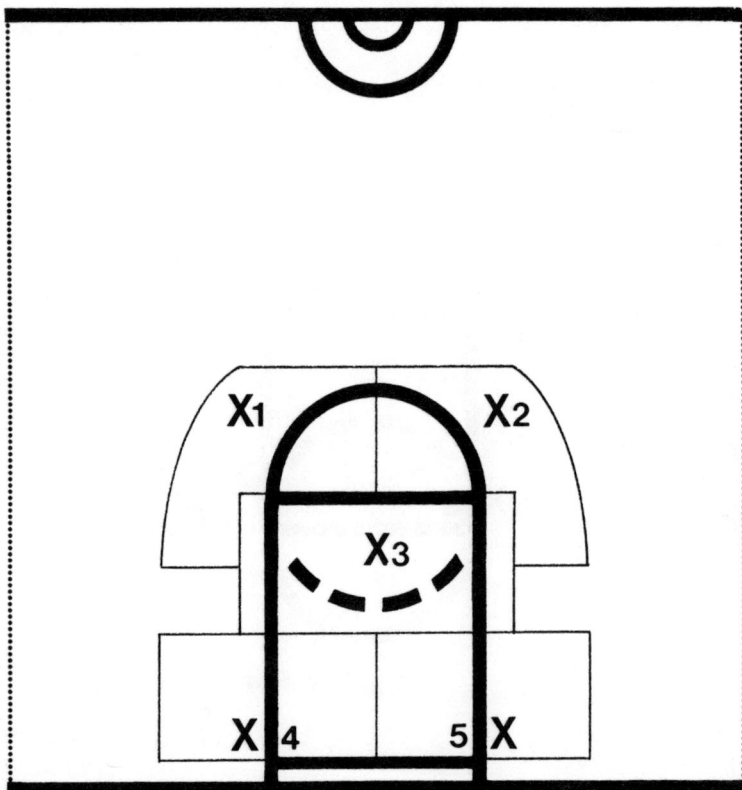

Illus. 47

As can be noted, each player's area overlaps the adjacent area. This is so that no area on the floor is left uncovered. Players are taught how far away from the basket the zone should cover but generally it is not farther out than 18-20 feet. If the ball is beyond that distance it is not covered by the defense.

Another example of a zone defense lines one player at the top of the circle, two in the middle of the lane and two at the baseline. This is called a 1-2-2 zone and is shown in Illustration 48 with player coverages indicated. In this zone, as in any, it is important that when the ball moves every player in the zone moves. A rule that helps players with this is: TRY TO KEEP YOUR ZONE THE SAME SIZE. When one side moves and the other does not, it makes the defense lopsided and creates "holes" or "gaps" for the offense to step into. A 1-3-1 and a 2-3 zone is also demonstrated in Illustrations 49 and 50.

Illus. 48

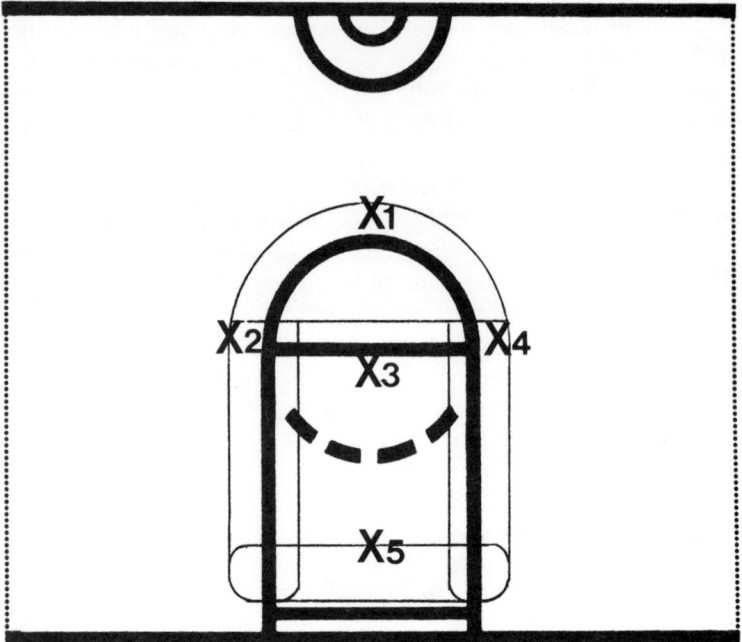

Illus. 49

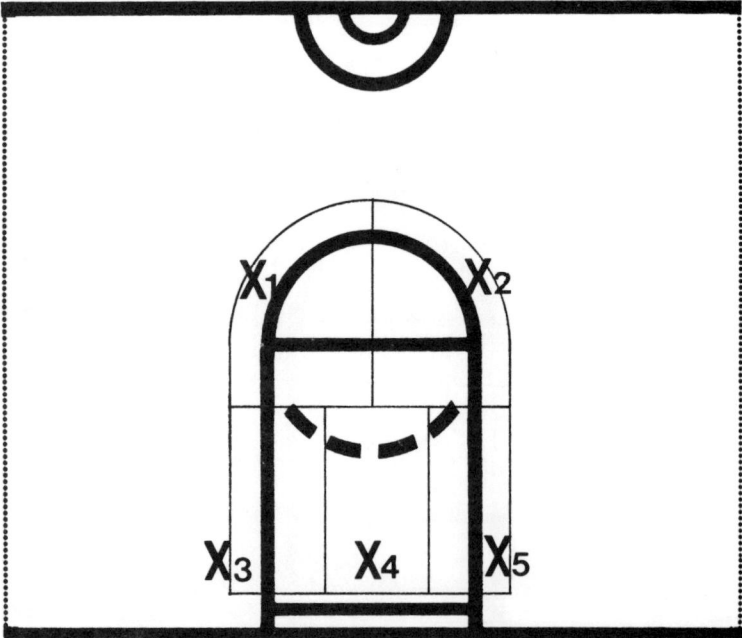

Illus. 50

The basic differences and similarities in **player-to-player** and **zone defenses** then are:

1. Player-to-player guards an individual player all over the court.
2. Zones guard the ball as it comes into assigned areas of the floor.
3. Player-to-player takes away the outside shot.
4. Zones take away the inside shot and allow the 18-foot shot.
5. Both focus on the ball.
6. Both use fundamental defensive skills.
7. Both demand verbal communication.
8. Both require aggressive tough players to make them successful.

Good defense is **half** the game of basketball. There is very little glory in it. It takes a well-conditioned, hard-working, ambitious player to play it, and does not have the glamour that scoring points has. But **played well,** it can bring much self-satisfaction to you from the game. **Played well,** it gives you pride in your contributions to your team, and **most of all** it can and does win basketball games. It is the secret to individual success as well as team success. It demands **all** that an eager young and older player alike possess. PLAY DEFENSE.

SECTION TWO

Offense:
The Secret to Survival

SECTION TWO

OFFENSE: THE SECRET TO SURVIVAL

Offense — the time during the game when your team has the ball — is one of the most "fun" times of every basketball game. This is when every player wants to do the most she can to help put the ball in the basket. There is a certain thrill to hearing and seeing the ball go through the net. There is an almost equal thrill in passing the ball that leads to a score.

The entire game's objective is, of course, to score more points than the other team. This requires players who can handle the ball well enough to be able to accomplish this objective.

Offensive skills can be divided into four basic categories — **dribbling, passing, shooting,** and **movements.** Nearly everything that happens on offense will fall into one of these categories. They are the types of skills that can be practiced without many players and their mastery depends on how many hours of hard work you are willing to give them.

It is also very important to recognize the significance of being able to execute these skills equally well with both hands. Many young players are content to practice only what they already can do and this usually does not include the non-dominant hand.

Offense is not a phase of the game that most players have to be prompted to practice. It is important, however, that you practice correctly and try to learn the skills as they will contribute to the game the most effectively. In the pages that follow the most basic of offensive skills will be discussed. Work on the fine points of each. You will find they will make you a much better offensive player.

THE DRIBBLE

Dribbling is the process of bouncing the ball in successive bounces with one hand at a time. The use of the dribble is a very misunderstood skill and as a result too much dribbling is often used in a game. The basic rule of dribbling is this: **DRIBBLE ONLY WHEN YOU CANNOT MOVE THE BALL WITH A PASS.** To stand in one spot and bounce the ball accomplishes very little and should not be done.

If, however, you do need to dribble, you should have several types of dribbles available to you.

LEFT AND RIGHT DRIBBLE

This is the most basic type of dribble and involves moving the ball up and down using a complete follow-through. The ball can be dribbled using a **control** dribble or a **speed** dribble. A **control** dribble is one that is used when guarded closely by the defense. It is a low dribble and one that is protected by your body.

A **speed** dribble is used when you want to get from one spot to another as fast as possible and you are not as closely guarded. The ball should be pushed out in front, then "caught up to" and pushed out again. You should not lose any speed if you push the ball out in front of you far enough to be able to run at full speed to catch it.

You should be able to execute the basic dribble with both right and left hand equally well before you proceed to the other types of dribbles. (Illus. 51 and 52)

Illus. 51

Illus. 52

CROSSOVER DRIBBLE

The crossover dribble is a control dribble which moves the ball quickly from one hand to another. It "crosses the ball over" from one hand to the other in an attempt to avoid defensive moves. The key to the success of this dribble is to use the **lower, quicker** bounce just before switching hands. When the defensive player **reaches** for the ball, the lower quicker bounce is used to put the ball under the defensive player's reaching hand. (Illus. 54)

Illus. 53   Illus. 54   Illus. 55

REVERSE DRIBBLE

This is also a control type of dribble and is used to keep the ball away from the defense by putting your **own body between** your **defense and the ball.** While dribbling forward, the dribbler pivots in either direction and puts the ball in the opposite hand while she has her back to

Illus. 56   Illus. 57   Illus. 58

the defense. By moving the ball to the other hand this allows the dribbler to change directions.

The reverse dribble is a useful dribble. It should be executed quickly, however, as it is not to the offense's advantage to have your back to the play long. Caution should be taken here also not to allow the ball to be stolen by **another** defensive player coming up on your **blind** side.

BEHIND-THE-BACK DRIBBLE

This is a control dribble that is a bit more difficult to execute but can be more useful than a reverse dribble in that it allows you to change direction and hands, keep your body between the ball and the opponent and still not turn your back on the play. (Illus. 59)

In this dribble the ball must be put behind the back on a bounce (Illus. 60) and recovered in order to change direction. If you are going to your right, dribble the ball in your right hand, put in behind your back and recover it in your left hand, going to your left after recovery. (Illus. 61) A hint that may help with this is to get into somewhat of a "sitting" position and you may find it easier to put the ball where you want it in order to change hands more easily. Long arms also help in doing this dribble.

Whatever dribble you find necessary to use in given situations, the following points apply to all:
1.   STAY LOW AND IN A READY POSITION.
2.   KEEP THE BALL AS FAR AWAY FROM THE DEFENSE AS POSSIBLE.
3.   WHEN GOING TO THE RIGHT, DRIBBLE WITH THE RIGHT HAND.
4.   WHEN GOING TO THE LEFT, DRIBBLE WITH YOUR LEFT HAND.

Illus. 59   Illus. 60   Illus. 61

5. KEEP THE DRIBBLE LOW — NEVER ABOVE THE WAIST — MORE TOWARD KNEE HEIGHT.
6. DRIBBLE WITH A PURPOSE AND NEVER WHEN YOU CAN PASS.

PASSING

If scoring is necessary for **survival**, then passing is necessary for scoring. Passing is really just as important for offense as is shooting. To give someone a pass that leads to two points can be a very satisfying skill.

There is no such thing as a good offensive player who is not a good passer. Learning to be a good passer requires the following ingredients:
1. Possessing a variety of passes you are able to use.
2. Knowing **when** to use what pass.
3. Learning to pass to an open space, into which a teammate is moving.
4. Learning to recognize passing lanes.

The next section deals with the **variety** of passes that you can learn and practice. The remaining three requirements will be discussed at the end of this chapter.

CHEST PASS

The **chest pass** is the most common of all passes. It can be used in a variety of situations and gives perhaps the most speed and force to any pass used. (Illus. 62)

The following techniques should be used with the chest pass.
1. Both hands should be evenly spread on the ball, one hand on either side of it.

Illus. 62

41

2. Extend arms outward with palms facing outward and full extent of reach.

3. Take a step into the pass. Use your legs; it will give the pass more speed.

4. Keep your elbows **in** — **don't** put them out like a chicken wing.

5. Follow through completely — that is, extend your arms with palms outward to their fullest extent.

Any time you can use a chest pass, you should. You have more control because you use both hands. Practice this pass every time you play.

BOUNCE PASS

(Illus. 63) The **bounce pass** is done with the exact same movements as the chest pass, except that the ball is put on the floor instead of in the air. Keep in mind the following:

1. Place hands on the ball as in chest pass — one on either side and spread out.

2. Extend arms and hands toward floor with palms facing out.

3. Bend knees and keep body low. This will help you to see the passing lane at this level as well as at a higher level.

4. Put some power into this pass or it is easily intercepted.

5. Pass the ball so that it bounces halfway between you and the receiver.

Illus. 63

42

OFF-THE-DRIBBLE PASS

(Illus. 64) This pass is done in the middle of a dribble. It is used when the passer does not have time to pick up the dribble and use both hands. It is necessary to be able to accurately throw this pass because you often see an open player while you are advancing the ball toward your basket and you need to get the ball to her immediately. To pass the ball off the dribble:

1. **As ball is brought up in the dribble,** push the ball toward the receiver either on a bounce or in the air.
2. Stay low in the dribble while you are executing this pass.
3. Follow through fully by extending your arms in a straight line toward the target. The **target** is the **receiver** if the ball is passed in the **air.** The **target** is the **floor halfway** between you and the receiver if the ball is **bounced.**

This is a fun pass to use and you feel a real sense of pride when you give your teammate an off-the-dribble pass quickly and accurately.

Illus. 64

BASEBALL PASS

(Illus. 65) This pass is passed in much the same way that you would throw a baseball. It is used to pass the ball long and fast and probably is seen more often in fast break situations than any time else.

To pass the baseball pass:

1. Bring the ball in **one hand** back close to your ear.
2. Bring elbow through first — **lead with it.**

Illus. 65

3. Follow through in full extension in direction of the target.
4. Use your legs by stepping into the pass. This will give thrust and speed to the pass.

It is important that you pass the ball more on a line drive than in a high arc to get the ball to your intended target as fast as possible. The **follow-through** becomes very significant for this pass in particular, as in all passes.

OVERHEAD PASS
(Illustration 66)

1. Place both hands on the ball, one on either side.
2. Bring both hands with ball straight up in the air over the head.

Illus. 66

3. Extend arms outward fully with palms out in the direction of target.

4. Be careful you do not bring the ball too far back behind the head.

5. Take a step in the direction of the receiver. This will help make the pass more accurate.

The overhead pass is used to pass the ball over a defender, especially one who is shorter than you. This pass, however, is misused and sometimes players try to pass the ball **through** the defender's hands. Obviously this cannot be done and you need to be sure that passing lanes are open enough to use this pass.

WHAT PASS WHEN

At the beginning of the passing section we stated that it was as important to know **what** pass to use **when** as it was to have the skill of various passes. The following are some brief rules that will help you to know what passes to use:

1. To get the ball inside — **BOUNCE PASS**
2. To get the ball long — **BASEBALL PASS**
3. From point to wing — **CHEST PASS** (except when closely guarded)
4. To lob or get ball over shorter opponent — **OVERHEAD PASS**
5. Quick pass to teammate on the move — **OFF-DRIBBLE PASS**
6. If there is a choice between two passes, use the one in which you have the most confidence.
7. Do not look directly at your target. Focus your eyes on the spot directly under the net whenever possible. It will help you see all open players.
8. Create openings with movement of the ball in fakes. A **FAKE** is going through all the motions of a pass without releasing the ball.

A **passing lane** is an **open** space between the ball and a potential receiver. When being defended, the areas by the defender's ears, sides, and through her legs are possible openings for the passer to pass the ball. The defender of the receiver, however, is also important to watch. If she can extend her arms and/or hands into the lane to touch the ball before it gets to your receiver, you do not have an open passing lane.

Receiving the pass is important to mention here. You should always be **moving** to meet the pass. Any time you are standing still on the court you are not helping as much as you could. Move **toward** the pass and **away** from the defense. When you see an open space, move into it.

If you have the ball and you **see** an open space look for one of your teammates to move into it and put the ball in the space with the appropriate pass.

Three basic rules of passing:

1. **LOOK INSIDE FIRST** — to see if someone is open close to basket.
2. **PASS TO A SPACE TO WHICH A PLAYER IS MOVING.**
3. **LOOK AT THE DEFENSE** — **yours** and the **receiver's** and pass away from the defense.

Follow these rules and perfect your passing skills and you will be on your way to becoming the complete offensive player.

SHOOTING

If offense is the secret to survival, **shooting** is the **backbone** of **offense.** From very early ages through old age people pick up basketballs everywhere and attempt to put them in baskets. Some merely throw the ball; others are serious shooters. Whatever may be the situation, the player who is working on her game will pay close attention to any and all pointers that will help make her a better shooter.

The main objective of basketball is to score points. You cannot **survive** in the game without scoring. It is vital that your team get the ball into the best **areas** on the floor for the most chance for success. These are called **percentage areas.** The ball-handling skills discussed previously are the means to do this.

Once the ball is in these areas, you will need to have **three main types** of shots that you can use effectively — **the layup, the outside or set shot,** and **the jump shot.** As the defense reacts to ball movement, you will know which type of shot to use when. This will be discussed at the end of this section.

Some **general** thoughts on shooting and practicing your shot include:

1. You are not **born** a good shooter. You have to **develop** this skill by hard practice.
2. Know your **target** area. When out **in front** of the basket it should be right **over the front of the rim.** When at an angle and within 5-10 feet, it should be the center of the backboard square. Concentrate each time you shoot to this area and make it a habit.
3. Do not shoot from **one** spot on the floor only. You should shoot from all around the basket within your range. Your **range** is the **distance from the** basket from which you can **score 40%-50% of the time.** Do not practice from farther out than

this. It contributes to many bad habits and will keep you from being a good shooter from anywhere. This is a **KEY** point.

4. Learn what these areas are. Do not guess. You can do this by shooting from all around the basket and discovering when you have to change your shot to get the ball there. If you have to do this you are probably out of your range. Each player's range will be different.

5. Learn the proper techniques so you can evaluate your own shot. For example, how your hands are placed on the ball, how you release the ball, etc.

6. You have to develop your own ''touch'' on the ball. This is the proper feel of the ball in your hands. It cannot be given to you by your coach but must be developed and recognized by each player.

If you will keep these points in mind as you practice the shots illustrated in the pages that follow, you will find you will make noticeable progress and will be on your way to becoming a consistent shooter.

LAYUPS

The **layup** is probably the highest percentage shot on the floor. It is shot on the move — toward the basket. Depending on the direction you are coming from, you will use different types of layups. A **right-hand** layup should be used approaching the basket from the right side. A **left-hand** layup is used approaching the basket from the left, while a **reverse** and **reach-back** can be used coming down the baseline from either the left or the right side.

RIGHT-HAND LAYUP
(Illustration 67 and 68)

To shoot a **right-hand** layup:

1. Approach the basket from the **RIGHT** side of the floor, dribbling the ball in your **RIGHT** hand.
2. When you get about halfway between the foul line and the basket, pick up the ball while on your left foot.
3. Take two steps — right, left.
4. Release the ball while going up on your left foot.
5. Extend your right arm fully and follow through toward the **TARGET** — which is the **CENTER** of the square on the backboard.
6. **KEEP YOUR HEAD UP AND YOUR EYES ON THE TARGET.**

Illus. 67

Illus. 68

Illus. 69

Illus. 70

Illus. 71

LEFT-HAND LAYUP
(Illustration 69, 70, and 71)

To shoot a **left-hand** layup:

1. Approach the basket from the **left** side of the floor, dribbling the ball in your **left** hand.
2. When you get about halfway between the foul line and the basket, pick up the ball while on your **right** foot.
3. Take two steps — left, right.
4. Release the ball while going up on your **right** foot.
5. Extend your **left** arm **fully** and follow through toward the **target** — the center of the square on the backboard.
6. **KEEP YOUR HEAD UP AND YOUR EYES ON THE TARGET.**

FRONT LAYUP
(Illustration 72)

This layup is shot from directly in front of the basket. To shoot a **front** layup:

1. Dribble the ball in your dominant hand down the middle of the floor.
2. When you get just beyond the foul line pick up the dribble while going up on your left foot.
3. Take steps — right, left — and release the ball at the top of your fully extended right arm.

Illus. 72

4. Follow through completely toward the **target — which is just over the top of the rim.**

Approaching the basket from the front allows the player to make up her mind whether to shoot the ball from the front, right, over the top of the rim or to put the ball against the backboard with the right hand on the right side or with the left on the left side. While any of these choices may be yours, you need to work on the front layup. It often is the quicker one to use.

REVERSE LAYUP
(Illustrations 73, 74 and 75)

This layup is shot from the side of the basket that is opposite the one from which the approach is made.

1. Dribble toward the basket on the left side of the floor with your left hand.

2. When you are nearly at the place where you would **release** the shot for a **right-hand layup,** pick up your dribble while on your left foot.

3. Take two steps until you are just past the basket — RIGHT — LEFT.

4. While on your left foot put the ball in your right hand and release it back over your head in somewhat of a ''hook'' shot fashion.

5. Extend fully and keep your head up and your eyes on the target which is the center of the square on the backboard.

Illus. 73   Illus. 74   Illus. 75

This layup is used by **right-handers** who approach the basket from the left side but who are not confident enough to use their left hand. You **can** shoot with your **right** hand on the left side but this is dangerous in that it makes you put the ball between you and the defense. Taking it to the other side of the basket protects the ball more.

The reverse layup can also be shot coming down the other side of the floor. The process described previously is merely reversed and the ball is shot with the left hand on the right side of the basket.

REACH-BACK

The difference between the **reach-back** and the reverse layup basically is that in the reach-back, if you **approach** from the **left** you **shoot** with the **left**. The opposite is true with the reverse. In the reverse you **approach** from the **left** and **shoot** with the **right** and **approach** from the **right** and **shoot left**.

The **reach-back layup** is **characterized** by the following points:

1. Approach the basket down the baseline.
2. Use a slight hesitation step when you reach the basket, then with a burst of speed go just beyond basket.
3. Reach back and shoot the ball with the hand you were drib-

Illus. 76   Illus. 77

bling with (right if coming from right (Illus. 76), left if from left). (Illus. 77)

4. You should be **facing** away from the baseline when you release the ball with a full extension.

5. Compare Illustration 75 with Illustration 77 to note the difference in body position and shooting hand with the **reverse** and **reach-back layups** on the same side of the floor. **The reverse faces the end line** and the **reach-back faces the foul line.**

The advantage of being able to shoot a **reach-back** layup is that you can execute a drive down the baseline, hesitate at the approach side of the basket (defense will make a move here to try and block the shot), then spurt to opposite side and keep ball in the same hand for protection. This puts the defense one or two steps behind because they have hesitated when you did.

All the layups that we have described are necessary for a complete offensive player to have at her disposal. All of these can also be done in a **power layup** manner. A power layup is done with few **if any** dribbles. You take the two steps that you allowed off an explosive move. The steps should be long and powerful. Power layups are used in fast break situations and when you have a clear open space to the basket and can build up speed. Do them with **AUTHORITY AND CONTROL.**

SET SHOT
(Illustrations 78, 79, 80, 81,and 82)

The shot that everyone seems to practice the most is the **set shot.** This is a shot when the player has time to stop and get ready or "set" before shooting the ball. The **technique** of shooting is **very** important. If you learn and practice incorrectly you will have less of a chance to become a consistent, accurate shooter. The following basic techniques of shooting should be used and checked frequently in your shot:

1. **BODY** — balanced and "squared to the basket." This means **facing the basket fully** and not with one side or the other toward it. This should be the position **every** time a shot is taken and should be checked carefully.

2. **FEET** — directly under the hips — not staggered to begin with but one placed before the other as the shot is taken.

3. **SHOOTING HAND** — fingers widely spread on ball — ball should rest on front and back pads of hands and should rest behind it.

4. **NON-SHOOTING HAND** — place on side of ball.

Illus. 78

Illus. 79

Illus. 80

Illus. 81

Illus. 82

53

5. **ELBOW** — place directly under ball and keep inside the plane of body.
6. **WRIST** — cock the wrist back — the ball should be placed on the hand with the wrist in much the same position as it would be if you were a waitress carrying a **tray**.
7. **EYES** — focused on the target during the entire shot.
8. Bring ball up right over forehead and extend **up** toward basket.
9. **FOLLOW-THROUGH** — ball should roll off middle finger last — hand should follow through completely — snapped forward (see Illus. 86). This provides the backspin that is necessary for the shot.

Practicing the shot should be a serious experience. That is, "shooting around" usually does not help you to become a better shooter but rather contributes to bad habits. Check frequently the points outlined above. Sometimes if you correct just one of them, your shot will improve.

JUMP SHOT
(Illustrations 83, 84, 85 and 86)

The jump shot is shot as a set shot with a jump put into it. As you bring the ball up for the shot, jump **straight up** with feet parallel and release the ball at the top of the jump. You should come down from the jump in the same spot from which you jumped.

The jump shot is the most effective shooting weapon in basketball. It helps you to be able to shoot off the move and thus gives you **more opportunities** to shoot. It is also the most difficult shot to defend against.

Do not try to shoot the jump shot at too great a distance from the basket. Start close (10-12 feet) or closer, and practice the form of the shot until that is learned. When you try to shoot **any** shot too far from the basket, you will form bad habits because you'll need to **get the ball there** and will do so any way you can. **Learn the shot first, before you move too far out** and practice from all around the basket.

While it is important to be able to shoot layups, set shots and jump shots, you also need to know which shot to shoot when. The following pointers may be of help as you become selective in your shooting:

1. Against player-to-player defense: The layups and close-in shots will be more common.
2. Always look for the jumper 10-12 feet off the drive or behind a screen or pick.
3. Use the appropriate layup with the correct hand as discussed.
4. When you have time to **set** and take your time — do so.

Illus. 83

Illus. 84

Illus. 85

Illus. 86

5. Stay square to the basket with all shots.
6. Determine your own percentage areas. To most players these are layups but sometimes pulling up within 6-8 feet without defense being so close becomes more of a percentage shot than a layup.
7. Zones do not usually give too many layup opportunities but they do often allow good outside shots.
8. The more types of shots you can shoot with consistency, the more shots you will get. If you can only shoot a **set** shot and dominant hand layup, you will be very limited in the number of shots you will get in a given ballgame.

Shooting is fun. It is the object around which the entire game is built. Practice every time you play. Work on the fundamentals of the shot. Be a **SERIOUS** shooter and help your team to reach the offensive goals they have set. **OFFENSE IS THE KEY TO SURVIVAL — SHOOTING IS THE KEY TO OFFENSE.**

INDIVIDUAL MOVES

While the game is played with five people on a team working together, it is basically built on each player's individual ability to perform certain skilled movements. This section deals with several of those fundamental movements. These are necessary to master before two- or nine-player movements can be used.

FAKING

Faking is moving in such a manner that you make the defense think you are going to do something but you do not do it. Fakes are used on **shots, passes, and cuts.** To fake properly, you must go through the complete motion of a move without actually making the move. For example, when using a **fake with a shot,** you go through the complete shooting movements without releasing the ball (of course this does not include **jumping** on the jump shot as this would be traveling.)

Faking when passing also involves completing the entire passing motion without releasing the ball. You have to make the defense react to your fake so that you can execute the desired movement. Faking while passing must be complete and quick for the desired reaction to result.

Faking while cutting involves your making a fake or a false step or movement in one direction to get the defense to react, and then moving in a different direction. The direction of your fake will depend on the direction you actually intend to move. If you always move in the same direction without ever using fakes, your defense will eventually "figure you out" and it will be more difficult for you to get opened. Faking should become a natural part of your list of offensive skills.

CUTTING

Cutting is a skill that involves your making a sharp move toward the basket or toward the ball. It requires a quick first step and usually includes a faked movement in one direction with an actual movement in the opposite or different direction. Sometimes these cuts describe a "V" pattern. Illustration 87 shows this pattern by O-*2* cutting sharply toward the basket then out toward the ball. O-*2* describes a "V" in her cut by cutting toward the ball, then toward the basket. It is a good point to remember to try and cut in a "V" pattern. Cuts should be **sharp, quick, and made frequently.** This keeps you **moving** all the time **when you do not have the ball** — a most important phase of the game. **Remember:** When you are **standing,** you are not **contributing.** Cuts are the main technique in helping you to contribute **offensively** when a teammate has the ball.

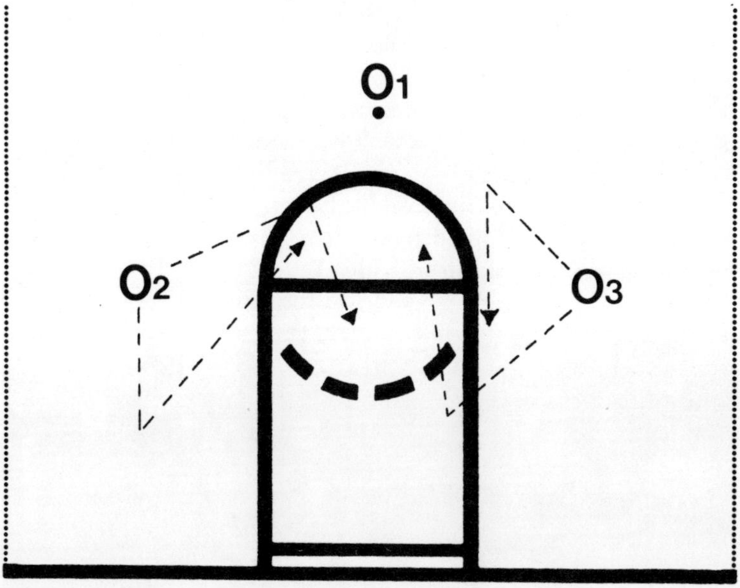

Illus. 87

PIVOTING

Pivoting can be done with or without the ball and is also used in blocking in defensive rebounding. It is the art of planting one foot and turning either part way or completely around.

When you are **dribbling** and come to a stop, you must determine which is your **pivot foot** — that is the foot that will remain stationary while the other one can move. In this fashion you can move to protect the ball from your opponent.

You can use a **reverse** pivot to turn your back on your opponent. In a reverse pivot, a step **away** from the forward direction is taken and the direction in which you are facing reverses. If you use a **reverse** pivot after you have come to a stop off a move and you have the ball, be sure to use a **two-step** stop. You then can use either foot as a pivot foot.

When you come to a two-step stop, you stop with both feet at a time — side by side. If you use a **one-step** stop, one foot stops in front of the other and the **back has** to be the pivot foot.

Learning to pivot correctly keeps you from traveling with the ball. It enables you to get around players more quickly and helps make the cuts you are using much more effective.

JAB STEP
(Illustration 88)

A **jab step** is used against your opponent when you are trying to get open for a shot or a drive. With the ball, before you have dribbled, take a forward step toward the defense, keeping your other foot as your pivot foot. The step should be decisive enough to make the defense react by taking a step back.

After the step is taken toward the basket, bring that foot back even with the other one. If the defense reacts by taking a step back, you can pull up and shoot **if you are within your** range. If the defense does not react back, jab again this time on the other side of her.

Illus. 88

ROCKER STEP

The **rocker step** is a combination of jab steps. The player takes a jab step forward with the non-pivot foot. The foot is then brought behind the pivot foot so that the body is sort of **rocked** back. Another jab step is taken and brought back. All this is done with the pivot foot stationary.

CROSSOVER STEP
(Illustration 89)

The crossover step is made by crossing the non-pivot foot in front of the body and placing it close to the defensive player's foward foot. At this time a drive to the basket is possible if you are close to the defensive player. A crossover dribble is used with this drive also. In order for this step to be effective, you have to get the defensive player close to you. If she is overplaying you to begin with, use a crossover step and go to the basket right away.

COMBINATIONS

The jab, rocker, and crossover steps are used mostly in combination with each other. Below are patterns possible in using these steps — possible defensive reactions are included;

1. Jab step (defense reacts back) pull up and shoot.
2. Jab step (defense does not react back) crossover step and drive.
3. Jab step (defense does not react back) rocker step (defense comes toward you) crossover and drive.
4. Rocker step back (defense does not come toward ball) jab-back and shoot.

Illus. 89

59

5.   Defense over playing — crossover and drive.

Of course all of these steps and reactions are done very quickly. These individual moves are really a type of **fake** until one of them leads to an actual move. They are important to practice faithfully. Start out slowly until you have the mechanism of each move down. Watch as many one-on-one contests as you can and notice one-on-one moves in games. These steps are there — sometimes so fast you cannot detect them but they are there and started just where you are.

PICKS AND SCREENS

Defense against picks and screens was discussed in the defensive section but from the offensive side it is important to know how to set picks and screens to make it difficult for the defense.

When you want to set a **pick** for a teammate, find the **leg** of her defensive player, **straddle it,** be as **wide** as you can, and hold your ground without sticking your knee out or fouling. Remember, it is **your** job to **set** the pick and your **teammate's** job to use it.

By this we mean once you've set the pick you cannot move into the path of a defensive player or lean into them. Your teammate must move in such a way that the defensive player has difficulty getting around you.

A **screen** is much like a pick but is not necessarily set right against a defensive play. When you set a screen, place your body in what you think will be the path of a defensive player. This can be set from behind the defensive player (back pick or back screen) in front or from the side.

The important thing to remember is that you can help "free up" your teammates by blocking the path of their defensive players. When you are on the court there is **always** something for you to be doing whether or not you have the ball. Players who look for opportunities to make things happen are the ones responsible for scoring, either directly or indirectly. Work to become one of those players.

TWO-PLAYER MOVES

In one form or other nearly all of basketball is based on two-player moves. That is, two offensive players combine in some way to set up a score. The three described below are the main three moves you will see and use in almost every basketball game.

GIVE AND GO

The **give and go** is the **most basic** two-player move in the game of basketball. It involves passing the ball to a teammate and making a cut to the basket in order to receive the pass back. You actually **give** the ball and go to the basket. (Illus. 90 and 91)

After the pass is made, you cut in one direction and go in the opposite direction, usually to the **inside** of your defensive player. Illustration 92 shows possible routes of the offensive player on the give and go.

(#1) **O**-*1* passes to **O**-*2,* jabs **outside** of **X**-*1*, then cuts **inside** of **X**-*1*. (Illus. 92)

(#2) **O**-*3* passes to **O**-*1*, jabs outside -**X**-*3*, cuts inside of **X**-*1*. (Illus. 93)

(#3) **O**-*2* passes to **O**-*1*, jabs outside of **X**-*2*, cuts inside of **X**-*2*. (Illus. 94)

(#4) **O**-*4* passes to **O**-*2*, jabs outside of **X**-*4*, cuts inside of **X**-*4*. (Illus. 95)

As can be seen, the **give and go** can be done from anywhere on

Illus. 90

Illus. 91

the floor. A good rule for you to follow is: **WHEN YOU PASS THE BALL, CUT TO THE BASKET FOR A RETURN PASS.** Work at this all the time. You'll be surprised at how often it succeeds if you work at it.

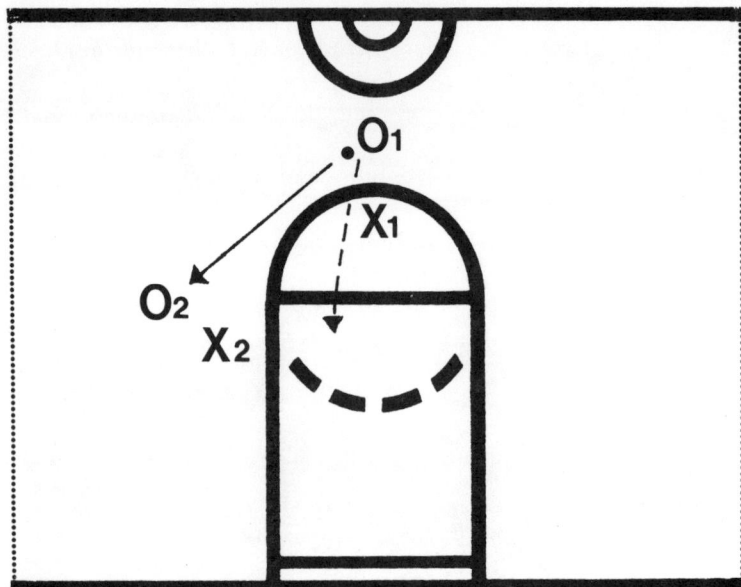

Illus. 92

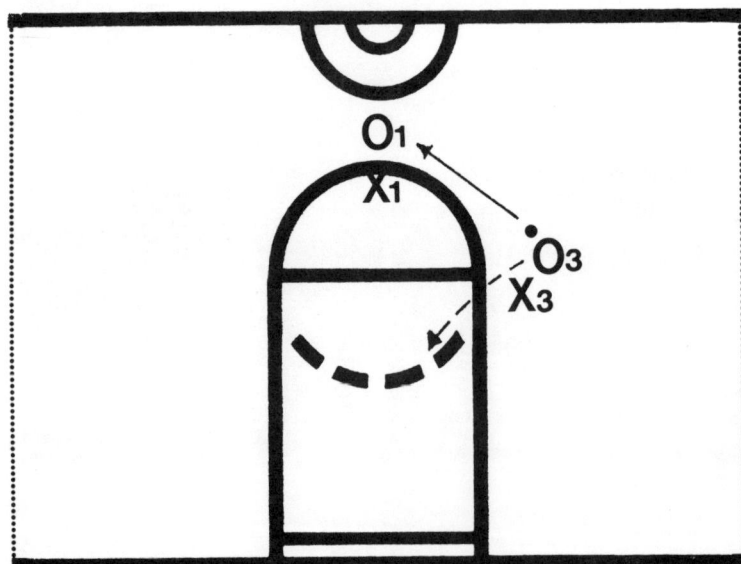

Illus. 93

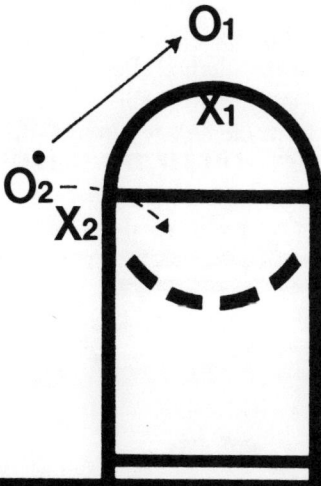

Illus. 94

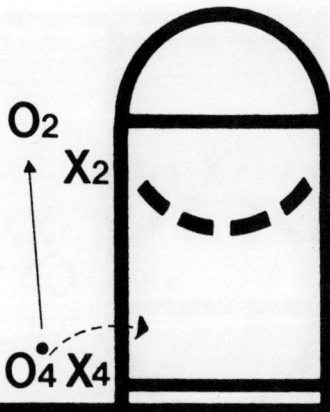

Illus. 95

PICK AND ROLL

In this two-player option, a pick is set and when the defense switches offensive players, the player who sets the pick rolls **to the inside** toward the basket for a return pass. In Illus. 96, **O**-*2* has the ball. **O**-*1* sets a pick on **X**-*2*, **X**-*1* and **X**-*2* (Illus. 97) change defensive assignments with **X**-*1* picking up **O**-*2* and **X**-*2* staying with **O**-*1*.

Because **switching** was the method chosen by the defense to defend the **pick,** the way to counterattack this is by the player who sets the pick (**O**-*1*) rolling to the inside for a return pass. REMEMBER: **THE OFFENSIVE PLAYER ONLY ROLLS IF THE DEFENSE SWITCHES.** If the defense uses **sliding through** or **going over the** top, there is no roll to the basket by the player who set the pick.

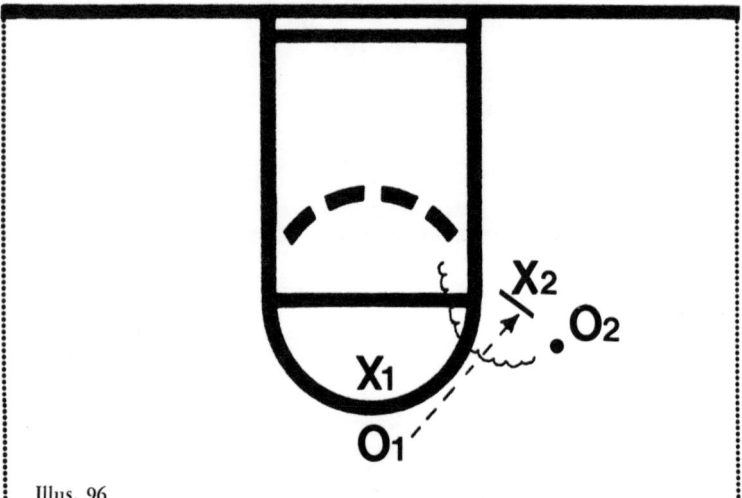

Illus. 96

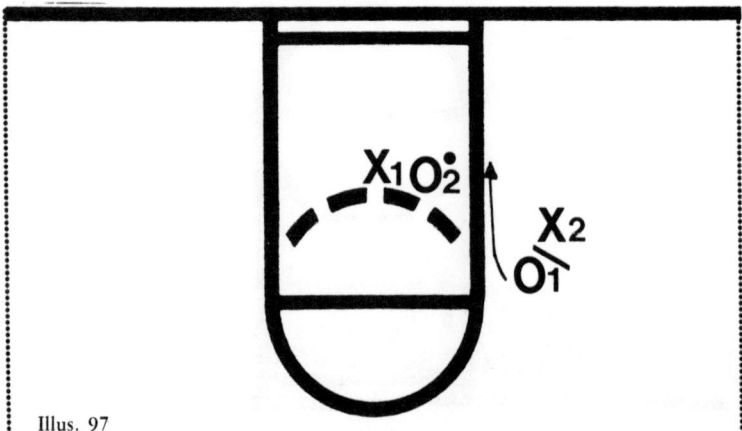

Illus. 97

BACK-DOOR CUT

The **back-door cut** differs from the give and go in that the cut is made **behind** the defensive player. In Illustration 98 you can notice the path of the player making the back-door cut.

(Illus. 99) **X-2** is overplaying **O-2**. **O-2** takes a jab step away from the basket and holds out a target hand to receive a pass. When the defense reacts toward the step, **O-2** cuts behind **X-2** (or back door) to receive a pass from **O-1**.

Back-door cuts can also be made all over the floor. The key to watch

Illus. 98

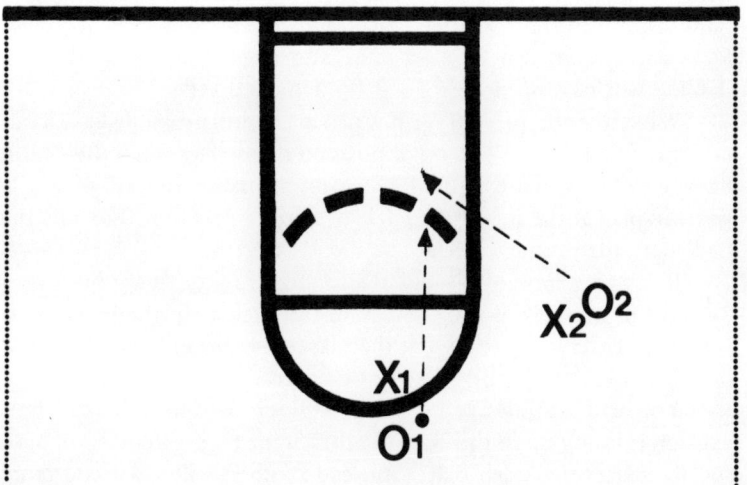

Illus. 99

for is **DEFENSIVE OVERPLAY** — defense playing too close. This gives the opportunity to go behind the defensive player and you find yourself wide open. The better offensive player you become, the more closely guarded you will be and the more back-door cuts you will be able to make.

Individual offensive skills all build on one another. Dribbling, passing, shooting, cutting all depend one on another. Be careful to give attention to **every** offensive skill and not to just the ones you enjoy or can do well. Every **team's** offense depends solely on how well **each player** can perform these skills. **Team offense will be only as good as individual offense.**

TEAM OFFENSE

Team offense is the system or patterns of movement that a coach chooses for her team to use. There are many that can be employed but the key to this is how best can the five players on the floor use the skills they have to score points for their team. This, of course, is the coach's decision and young players should work as hard as they can to execute the offensive patterns the best they can.

Against **zone defense** your team offense will be different than against **player-to-player.** **Zone offense** will be organized so that outside shots are made possible. There will be fast passing, very little dribbling and movement through the zone defense. But probably most of the shots taken will be from outside the zone.

Player-to-player offense will have shots taken from the **inside** because each player will be guarded by one other player. Movement patterns on the court will have two- and three-player plays in them. Picks and screens will be used more and teams playing against this defense will have to possess good fundamental skills.

Whatever offense your team is playing, it will probably have a certain way for players to line up or position themselves when their team has the ball. If you are a **guard** — usually a smaller, quicker player — you will play at the top of the circle or at the side and will handle the ball more than other players.

If you are a **forward** — taller than a guard, a little slower but strong — you will play at the wing or side of the circle or at the baseline. If you are a **center** — the tallest of the players — you will play down low or in the lane with your back to the basket.

You will not **always** be in these positions but you may find yourselves lining up in this way initially. Some team offenses will have specific places that each player moves to, others will allow you more freedom to go where you want. Learn to recognize offensive movement by watching games and figuring out the patterns of play. Pick out one or two players and watch what they do to see if you can see a pattern.

Offensive basketball is exciting to watch and even more exciting to play. A team that is able to score a lot of points is the type of team everyone likes to watch. You can be very good defensively and keep a team from scoring but eventually it will become obvious to every player that **offense is the secret to survival** in a basketball game. You could keep a team to zero points but you cannot survive if **you** do not score.

Work on your offensive skills. Determine your strengths and your weaknesses and be serious and determined to work on both. Some of the drills and activities in the next section may be of help as you try to work on your own.

SECTION THREE

Practice:
The Secret to Skill

PRACTICE: THE SECRET TO SKILL

The previous sections have outlined specifically the fundamental skills necessary to become an effective basketball player. **Knowing** what these are and **understanding** them **mentally** is a vital link in being able to perform them. However, obviously this is not enough and no one is "born" a basketball player. This is **learned** activity as is almost everything else.

You will find a tremendous positive relationship between how much you practice these skills and how good you are as a player. Those skills practiced the most will be those skills at which you are the most proficient. **Practice,** then, becomes the secret to skill development.

Because of this important aspect of the game of basketball, this section will be devoted to all areas of practicing the game, emphasizing mainly ways that you can practice on your own. Before you begin your practice schedule or routine, however, there are two things you need to be aware of and plan for prior to each practice time — **equipment** and **warming up.**

EQUIPMENT

Unlike more elaborate and expensive individual sports, basketball demands very little equipment. This is one aspect of the sport that has helped it to become so popular. It will not cost much to learn to become a basketball player.

SHOES — The most important part of the player's body is her **feet;** therefore, the most important piece of equipment will be your **shoes.** Be very careful that you select **heavy** basketball shoes. There are many different kinds on the market and your local sporting goods dealer can help you find the pair that can meet your needs.

Some young players like the high top type of shoe because these can provide a bit more ankle support. However, the most important thing to remember here is to **be consistent** with the kind that you wear. In other words, don't wear high tops one day and low cuts the next.

The upper composition of basketball shoes comes in canvas or leather and both are adequate, depending on your preference. Canvas is sometimes selected over leather for high tops because of cost and also because some authorities believe that canvas conforms more to the shape of the foot. In reality, the choice between the two becomes a very personal one.

The main thing is to select a shoe with good arch support, a durable material for the upper shoe, and soles with good traction. Heavy shoes are necessary, in part, because of the friction that takes place while playing the game. Blisters are common and the proper shoes can help prevent and control this problem.

Remember: **DO NOT WEAR TENNIS SHOES OR STREET GYM SHOES TO PLAY BASKETBALL.** Try to keep your basketball shoes for just that: to play basketball in. Do not wear them for other activities. You will find this to be a helpful hint in both the care and wear of your shoes.

SOCKS — Because care of the feet is so important, another item of equipment necessary for the serious basketball player is **socks. ALWAYS WEAR TWO PAIRS OF SOCKS** when you play or practice the game. One pair should be cotton — the pair next to your feet or that you put on first. The other pair should be heavier sweat socks.

Wearing two pairs of socks helps to prevent blisters and aids in controlling the friction that takes place between the floor or court, your shoes, and your feet. Socks should be clean, should not be put on wet or damp, and should be free from holes and overuse. It is easy sometimes in your haste to get on the court to overlook putting on two pairs of socks. It is important that it become as much of a habit with the serious basketball player as it is to pick up your basketball before starting to play.

BALL — Although everyone who wants to learn to play basketball does not have to have her own ball, it is helpful if you do have one. If you play outside, a rubber basketball is satisfactory. These cost very little in comparison to leather balls.

Even though a leather ball is better to use on indoor courts than rubber ones, it certainly is not necessary to purchase a leather basketball. Be sure, however, that the ball you do use is regulation size.

The only other piece of equipment you need is a backboard and hoop. You can either purchase one for your own house or probably find some available at playgrounds or schools.

WARMING UP

Before you start playing or practicing each time you should "stretch out." Special attention should be given to the muscles and joints in your legs as this is the area of the body used the most vigorously by a basketball player. The following are examples of stretching exercises to be done before practice:

1. **Toe Touch and Hold** — Stand erect with knees locked. Reach down, touch toes and hold 3-5 seconds. Cross right leg over left and repeat. Cross left leg over right and repeat.

2. **Quad Stretch** — Stand erect and grasp right ankle bringing lower leg up to touch buttocks. Hold 3-5 seconds and repeat with other leg.

3. **Groin Stretch** — Sit with back erect and put soles of feet together. Press both knees toward the floor with each hand. The object is to stretch the area so that the legs will both touch the floor flat.

Other types of warmup activities might include light jogging, rope jumping, jumping jacks or other exercises which would include running or jumping activities.

INDIVIDUAL PRACTICE

Whereas basketball is a **team** game played with **five** players on a team, most of the skills needed to play the game are individual skills.

It's fun to play "pick up" games and necessary for overall development as a player, but sometimes the only person you have to practice with is yourself. Often players practice only shooting by themselves because they don't know anything else to practice.

The drills listed and described below are practice activities that you can do with just yourself and a minimal amount of equipment. You will find that faithful practice of these will improve your overall basketball skill.

PRACTICING DEFENSE

1. **Rope Jumping** — Jumping rope can be a great activity for improvement of overall conditioning and also foot work. A suggested plan would be for you to jump at least 5 minutes every day and during that 5 minutes to jump in various ways,

i.e. both feet, left foot, right foot, alternate foot, with a jump between jumps, changing paces.

2. **Power Jumps** — Pick a spot on a backboard, if available, and explosively jump 10 times to try and touch that spot, first with one hand, then with both hands. Jump from a set position and also taking a step or two.

3. **Defensive Slides** — Do a series of defensive slides down a selected line on a floor or if you are not on a basketball court you can do this on a sidewalk or in your garage. Assume a defensive stance, stay low and slide sideways leading with your forward foot. Change directions during the drill. DO NOT CROSS YOUR FEET IN THIS DRILL.

4. **Stutter Stepping** — In a low defensive stance begin to move your feet up and down in one place as rapidly as you can. Each foot should just clear the ground. Run as fast as you can for 10 seconds, rest 10 seconds and repeat. Do this for 10 repetitions. This is a great conditioning activity as well as a footwork drill.

5. **Shadow Defense** — Pretending you are guarding an opponent from the top of the circle, practice taking a step back with your inside foot. Think about whether or not the ''player'' has picked up her dribble and go through the defensive moves you make in playing defense. Remember to stay low and take a step back, using your hands. Practice the same drill at the baseline, taking a step back and moving to straddle the baseline.

6. **Quick Hands Drill** — In a low defensive stance, slap your hands against the outside of your own knees as fast as you can. Touch your hands to your chest, then to your knees. Do this as rapidly as you can. It will remind you to use your hands in defense.

PRACTICING OFFENSE

Dribbling

1. **Blind Dribbling** — In one place stand and dribble the ball first with your right hand, then your left while **keeping your eyes closed.**

2. **Zigzag Dribble** — Dribble first to your right, then to your left, defining a ''Z'' path. Be sure you change hands each time you change directions. If you have a pair of blinders do this drill as well as the rest of them wearing the blinders.

3.   **Stop-and-Go Dribble** — Start dribbling fast, slow up, then fast again. Change direction while you're doing this and be sure to change hands each time you change direction. Be sure to stay low and protect the ball while you are dribbling.

4.   **Combination Dribble** — Start dribbling forward in your right hand, change to your left using **crossover** dribble. Do a **reverse** dribble going from right to left and from left to right. Continue forward with right and left hand. Do a **behind-the-back** dribble going both directions and continue on down the floor. These should be done smoothly from one hand to the other and as fast as possible.

5.   **Dribble Series** — Dribble with:
   A.   dominant hand
   B.   weak hand
   C.   chest high and hard
   D.   as low as possible
   E.   around each leg in a figure 8
   F.   with two balls, first alternating, then together
   G.   machine gun: get into a low position with legs apart a little more than shoulder width. Begin an alternating dribble with left and right hand. Bring each hand around its respective leg and dribble with the hand behind the leg. The hands must move rapidly in front, in back and alternately. The key element is keeping the ball in the middle between the legs and low.
   H.   The sitting dribble:
      — with dominant hand
      — with weak hand
      — under the legs
      — behind the back
      — while doing situps
      — with two balls
   I.   Reaction dribble:
      — Bounce the ball and clap the hands in front and back before catching.
      — Standing erect, bounce the ball between the legs and catch it behind the body. Bounce it back between the legs and catch it in front. The bounce should be hard and quick.
      — Toss the ball into the air and clap as many times as possible before catching it.

6.   **Obstacle Dribble** — Set up chairs the length of a court and

dribble in and out of the chairs for time. Be sure to use both hands and keep the ball in the hand farthest from the chair around which you are dribbling. You can also use all the types of dribbles for this and can set up the chairs across the **width** of the court as well as the length.

Passing

1. **Flat Wall Passing** — Using a solid wall, and standing behind a marked line (can be any distance from wall but make it realistic to the distances you will be passing in a game), pass the ball against the wall so that it rebounds to you about chest level. Use all kinds of passes. Mark an area on the wall — a square or a circle and attempt to pass into that area. This drill is also excellent in helping you to **receive** the pass.

2. **Barrel Passing** — Cut a barrel in half longways and put the flat side up on a wall. Pass the ball against the curved side of the barrel and receive the pass off the barrel. This makes the ball come off at different angles. You can also designate a target on the barrel that you want the ball to hit.

3. **Tire Pass** — Hang a tire from a rope and try to pass through the tire. If you hang it directly in front of a wall, the ball will rebound back to you if you hit the opening. After you have mastered hitting the opening of the tire while it is stationary, swing the tire and attempt to hit it while it is moving.

4. **Passing Long** — This drill is used mainly to work on the baseball pass. Designate a line with a baseball pass. You can also use the wall for your target if facility arrangement permits.

5. **Fake and Pass** — Using a wall as a rebounder, fake a pass in one direction or with one type of pass and pass in another direction or use a different type of pass. Pass off a dribble, staying low and getting the pass off quickly.

6. **Dribble and Pass** — Combine any of the dribbling drills with the wall passing. For example: dribble around the obstacles for time to the line marked for passing. Pass through the tire or to a marked space on the wall until you have hit the space a predetermined amount of time.

Shooting

1. **Spot Shooting** — Select 5-7 spots 10-12 feet around the basket. Take 5 shots from each spot using first a set shot, then a jump shot.

2. **Shoot to Yourself** — Being very careful to use proper technique, get into your shooting position and "shoot" the ball straight up in the air being careful to follow through completely. This is an excellent drill to begin each day and practice with because it makes you really work on the fundamentals of the shot without being concerned if the ball goes in the basket.

3. **Alone Layup** — Starting from the right side at the free throw line extended:
   A. dribble in hard to the basket and shoot a right-handed layup
   B. rebound the ball
   C. dribble with the left hand to the left free throw line extended
   D. do a reverse dribble
   E. dribble to the basket with the left hand
   F. shoot a left-hand layup
   G. rebound the ball
   H. dribble with the right hand to the right side free throw extended.

Repeat this entire drill using each type of layup, i.e. reverse, front, reach-back. Do this drill for 2-3 minutes — Good conditioning drill as well as shooting drill.

4. **Rebound Shooting** — If you have access to a toss back (piece of equiment that is rigged like a trampoline but is upright — you pass the ball against and it rebounds back to you), pass the ball against it and shoot immediately upon receiving the pass back. Be sure you square to the basket before taking the shot. If you do not have a toss back, you can use a wall if it's situated so that this drill can be done.

5. **Off-a-Bounce Pass** — Backspin the ball on a bounce so that you can pick it up as if it were a bounce pass to you and shoot. Always try to be moving before you shoot. Practice shot faking also. Some general pointers about shooting include.
   A. **Practice technique** every day by shooting to yourself, to a partner or wall, or close in — right under or next to basket. This is the only time when you should be shooting while standing still.
   B. Do not practice shots you will not take in a game, i.e., 50-footers or 25-30-footers. Your technique will change and you are wasting your time.
   C. Except for No. 1 above, always be on the move prior

to shooting either off a dribble, off a pass, or just turning to square. This is a very important aspect of shooting practice.

D. Learn to use the glass or backboard when shooting at an angle and from 0 to 5 or 6 feet out. In other words, **when you can bank, do so.**

E. Practice mentally as well as physically — while you are shooting and at other times. **Think** about the techniques of the shot and go through it in your mind.

F. **When practicing free throws** — (1) to really work on the fundamentals of the shot and get the "feel" of the shot or to get into a "rhythm or groove" shoot 20-25 in a row and (2) to practice game-like shooting, shoot one or two, back away from the line or go to a different basket and shoot one or two more etc.

G. TRY TO MAKE SHOOTING **PRACTICE** AS MUCH LIKE A GAME AS POSSIBLE.

INDIVIDUAL MOVES

These moves, of course, include jab, crossover, rocker steps, faking, and pivoting. To practice them, you do not need another person — at least at first. Even after you've learned them fairly well and they have become habit to you, it is good to practice them without defense.

For the steps (jab, crossover, rocker) pretend you have a defensive opponent and go through each step. Execute drives, shooting layups and pulling up and shooting. Try them by themselves and in combination with each other.

Faking can be practiced in front of a mirror or just on the court with a ball. Remember to keep in mind that you go through the complete motions of the skills — passing, shooting, without releasing the ball. A good fake makes the defense behave and **react** to your fake.

Pivoting should be practiced with and without the ball. Standing still, turn around by moving one foot and keep the other stationary. Pivot on both feet going **front** and **reverse**. Practice off a dribble and off a move without the ball.

Perhaps the biggest mistake players make when playing is that they think playing is **practicing.** This is not always true. If you do not **practice correctly** and practice the correct skills, all the playing in the world will only perpetuate bad habits. Remember:

Practice Regularly • Practice Correctly • Practice Mentally

2794

CONDITIONING ACTIVITIES

The well-conditioned player will have a noticeable and decided advantage over one who is not well-conditioned. While practicing the drills discussed previously **contributes** to conditioning, it does not take care of all the training you need to do to be physically ready to play the entire game of basketball.

There are many different kinds of programs in which you can engage but there are few, if any, activities that can take the place of **running** to get you ready to play. The following is a suggested type of running program **during the summer** to help get you in condition:

1. Run or jog 1-3 miles each day.
2. Keep a record of the time it takes to jog each day.
3. Jump rope 5 minutes each day.
4. Swim whenever you can and record that also.
5. Play one on one, three on three, or five on five whenever you can. Try to play with players who are **better** than you are.

During the school year, or season if you play on a school team, the conditioning program will be much different. It will consist of:

1. **Short distance sprints** — i.e., 110s, 220s, 440s with rest in between each.
2. **End lines** — there are sprints on a basketball court when you sprint end line to end line and repeat before resting.
3. **Rope jumping** as fast as you can for 30-40 seconds with rest in between.
4. **Drills** — many of the drills you will do in practice will be conditioning type drills and if you work as hard on them as you should, they will improve your level of competence.

Practice is definitely the secret to your skill development. Your **attitude** toward this phase of the whole game becomes vital to your practice regularity. **If you practice carelessly, you will play carelessly.** You will find that you can achieve great satisfaction in **knowing** that you have worked as hard as you can to become a good player. Even if there are others who are better, and there will be, **doing the most you** can do **to become all that you can** will bring you great rewards as you play the exciting game of basketball.